April 20, 2003

May you find comfort in the love of others

Geneva Woehler

Geneva Woehler
7353 Rowena St
San Diego, CA
92119

*PRECIOUS MEMORIES:
HOW THEY LINGER*

PRECIOUS MEMORIES: HOW THEY LINGER

Geneva Smith-Woehler

VANTAGE PRESS
New York

FIRST EDITION

All rights reserved, including the right of
reproduction in whole or in part in any form.

Copyright © 1997 by Geneva Smith-Woehler

Published by Vantage Press, Inc.
516 West 34th Street, New York, New York 10001

Manufactured in the United States of America
ISBN: 0-533-12108-6

Library of Congress Catalog Card No.: 96-90617

0 9 8 7 6 5 4 3 2 1

To the memory of my husband
Wally
who, after death,
inspired me to write
and to find my way back home

Precious memories
    How they linger,
How they ever flood my soul.
            In the stillness of the
                    midnight,
        Precious, sacred scenes unfold.

Contents

Foreword xiii
Acknowledgments xv

March 10, 1995   1
August 1963   2
   First Embrace   4
March 11, 1995   5
   The Night before Saturday   8
May 1993   9
March 1995   10
   Sky Show   13
March 12, 1995   14
March 13, 1995   15
May 7, 1965   16
   Suit of Blue   17
March 15, 1995   18
March 18, 1995   18
Mother's Day 1965   19
   Mother's Day   20
March 19, 1995   21
March 20, 1995   22
March 25, 1995   25
March 30, 1995   26
April 9, 1995   26
April 1995   29
   Wally's Poem   30
May 8, 1995   31
   This House   34
   Tulips   36
May 1995   37
June 1, 1995   38

June 5, 1995	38
June 7, 1995	39
April 1958	39
June 8, 1995	39
Last Farewell	40
June 12, 1995	41
Our Fathers	43
July 1996	44
September 18, 1995	45
September 19, 1995	46
The General	47
September 27, 1995	49
Celebration of Life	50
October 1995	51
Autumn	52
October 25, 1995	53
Heaven's Call	53
November 1995	55
Thanksgiving Day	55
Thanksgiving	56
December 1995	57
Christmas Day	58
Silent Night	59
December 30, 1995	60
Auld Acquaintance	61
January 1, 1996	62
January 18, 1996	63
Vows Unspoken	64
February 10, 1996	65
February 14, 1995	65
February 12, 1965	66
February 13, 1996	66
To My Valentine	67
February 14, 1996	68
March 1, 1996	69
March 11, 1996	69
Better to Have Loved	70
To My Beloved	70

April 1996	71
June 9, 1996	72
Forget Me Not	74

Foreword

I was eighteen years old and working at my first job when I met Wally. He was married at the time and had four children. I didn't know him very well, but he seemed nice and always had a smile on his face. Within that first year at Aerojet, Wally's wife (of five years) and her daughter were killed in a tragic automobile accident. Shortly after his return to work, we shared casual conversation whenever he passed by my desk. In his need to talk to someone, we became good friends.

Within two years, our friendship had grown, we were married. We spent the next thirty years together raising our family of three boys. In 1990, Wally's medical problems began. He was diagnosed with a kidney disease, which was in remission a year later. In 1993 he suffered a mild heart attack while on a cruise to the Panama Canal. Finally, in 1994 the kidney disease returned in full force. As he started dialysis treatments, the clock began to tick. A kidney transplant was needed and we began testing immediately for a match. Although I was told I had a better chance of winning the lottery than being a match, I insisted on being tested along with our sons. As each son was eliminated, I became the last hope. At last the call came—I was his match!

From the moment we got word of the match, we began preparing for the surgery Wally would need in order to survive. After so many tests, numerous setbacks, and delays, we had a surgery date of March 29, 1995.

On March 10 we made an unscheduled trip to the hospital. Wally was ill and needed emergency medical care. However, I was certain that the doctors would have his condition back under control and we would stay on track for the surgery. Instead, he began to weaken as his ability to fight the illness failed. On the evening of March 11, 1995, Wally died.

Having thirty years of marriage end so abruptly by death was a terrible shock to me. I had never had anyone as close to me die. I tried comparing Wally's death to a divorce, because I knew of more people who had lost a mate through divorce than by death. However, I knew that divorce was usually a mutual departure and could often be bitter. Our separation was neither and left me struggling with so many different emotions. To who and where, could I turn to for comfort? Wally was always the one there for me. I suddenly had to deal with what seemed like an eternal pain in my heart and become the one person others depended upon to help ease their pain. Where was God now, where was He yesterday when we needed Him the most?

To who and where do I turn—so many questions without answers:

"Why did he have to die now when we were so close to surgery? Would surgery have made a difference? Why did God provide me with a kidney match but not the opportunity to help save his life? Where is he? Is he okay? Can he see me? Does he visit me? Is he happy with what I am doing?"

I was frantic to find answers to all these questions and began reading about death, grieving, and the hereafter. I desperately needed to talk to someone who had gone through the same experience I was going through—"the loss of a spouse."

In writing this book, I hope to help others deal with their grief during the loss of a loved one and tell them that they are not alone. While I am still going through the process myself, I am further along than I ever dreamed possible. With the help of friends, family, and some personal determination, I am making it back. If I can reach out and help just one person who might be experiencing what I did, then my mission will be fulfilled.

Acknowledgments

Wally was my best friend. I admired and looked up to him. He had so much patience with me. I thank him for taking this shy, unsophisticated, scared nineteen-year-old and transforming her into a mother, wife, and adult. Because of our thirty years together, I have the insight, strength, determination, and courage to compose my thoughts and share my feelings on a subject that is private and haunting; a subject that I still cannot let go of, "his death."

Gratitude to my sons, Michael, Christopher, and Robert for standing by me throughout this tragedy and letting me share my feelings and thoughts. Many times they put their pain aside to be there for me. My daughter-in-law, Martha, who has been my close companion each day; my future daughter-in-law, Marissa, who is new to our family but came forward with love and compassion; and my dear grandchildren, Eli, Tara, and Kyle who will miss their grandfather and who share my pain.

Thanks for my sister, Teresa, and sister-in-law, Debbee, for all the hand-holding, nose-wiping, and giving of their time by staying with me overnight and then taking turns calling me every night for weeks. To wonderful and caring family members who encouraged me to pick myself up and go on, that I was important to them.

A special thank you to my supervisor, Judy Beck, who stood by me prior to and throughout Wally's illness –his first diagnosis of kidney disease; his heart attack; renal failure; and, ultimately, his death. She knew when to send me home, when to let me be, when to push me forward, and when to offer advice. She is a very special person in my life and was much admired by Wally.

To my coworkers for putting up with my many moods and encouraging me to publish my writings.

To Wally's coworkers, who, after losing a friend, embraced me with kindness and thoughtfulness.

And thanks to my therapist, Cyndee, for walking with me and

showing me the path I must take to start a new life—one that I was resisting with all my heart and soul.

*PRECIOUS MEMORIES:
HOW THEY LINGER*

March 10, 1995

As we leave the house, I notice how dark blue the sky has become. It has been a rainy, dreary day with more rain in the forecast. There are so many clouds in the sky. They are so majestic—white, puffy, softly floating, and forever changing shapes as they follow us to our destination. I wonder if I will ever bring you back home again. Are you scared, too? You are so quiet as we drive through all too familiar streets—we have made this same journey many times before.

When we arrive at the hospital emergency room, everyone is so attentive. After numerous blood tests and X rays, you are admitted. The doctor tells me you have a 50-50 chance of survival—you have a serious infection. I can't believe that I am hearing him correctly. You seemed fine except for a high fever and a cough, and the pain in your abdomen can only be a bout of diverticulitis. What went wrong?

When I came home to take you to a specialist because of abdominal pain, you said you felt fine but might have a slight fever; it was 102 . We thought it was the diverticulitis, but with surgery so close, your doctor wanted you to see a specialist to make sure it wasn't anything more serious. How could this happen? We are too close to lose you now. I must get you to the hospital immediately.

As I sit here with you, I wonder if you are aware of what is happening, and I'm so afraid you will tell me you won't be going home with me—I am so scared. The doctor has ordered the dialysis team to come to your room to give a treatment. I am puzzled—you had a successful four-hour treatment earlier this morning. They assure me the X rays show no fluid in your lungs. I can only trust that they know what is best for you. I reluctantly leave you because there isn't enough room for me and all the equipment in your room.

Once I return home, I am restless and find myself trying to keep busy until you call to tell me they are finished and I can return to be with you. The sky is now becoming ominously foreboding. Upon my return you seem worse and the doctor has ordered mechanical breathing treatments. You have been on oxygen, but you just can't seem to get your breath. Your fever has returned, and I ask the nurse for permission to give you an alcohol rub. As I try to get your fever down, I pray with all my heart and soul that all of this will go away; the fever will break, the pain will subside, and your breathing will return to normal. After all, this is a hospital—you couldn't be in better care. At 10:30 P.M. you tell me to go home and get some sleep, you seem to be better; fever is down a little, and you aren't as anxious.

I cannot bear to leave you alone, but know you will worry about me if I stay. Maybe if I leave, you will get some rest and start getting better. Driving home, memories of our life together come flooding in; do you remember when we met? This could not end this way, not now, we need more time.

August 1963

The year is 1963—I am almost nineteen, my first job; I don't know you very well, but you are friendly and always have a smile on your face. My first impression is of someone kind and gentle, yet fun-loving and caring. You always ask how I am doing and seem genuinely interested in my response. That first Christmas you gave all the secretaries a bottle of perfume. Mine was a bottle of "My Sin." You probably don't know this, but I still have it; you made me feel special.

Coming to work one morning, I overhear one of the secretaries on the phone telling someone about a terrible accident. Somehow I know it has something to do with you. We have hardly spoken in the short time I have worked here—you are a big tease and I am so bashful that I have never said more than hello to you, but I felt something unexplainable at the time. I stopped to ask what had happened and was told your wife and daughter had been killed in an automobile accident. I am horrified. How could God take a mother and child, both so young? (Pat was only 29 and Michele was 9.) How could something this bad happen to someone as nice as you? What will you do now? How will you cope? What can I do?

That same weekend our family left for Tennessee for a visit. All I could think about while I was away was what you must be going through. What would happen when you returned to work; would you be the same kind, gentle person? How could you be?

After your return, I am so sorry for you, but I have no clue as to what to say, so I say nothing. Our friendship begins when you stop at my desk during breaks and talk to me about Pat. I mostly listen and let you tell me as much as you feel comfortable with, and each day seems to become easier for you. I enjoy our chats immensely, and it is nice having you as my friend. I am so young and you are so mature; I am so naive and you are so sophisticated; you enjoy teasing me and I get embarrassed so easily; I just can't imagine life without you, my friend.

Our friendship is very special and important to me. I enjoy your company and sometimes wish I were older, then maybe you would see me as a "woman" instead of a silly schoolgirl. I am so in awe of you; are you just being kind? How unfair life can be and I must stop torturing myself with unattainable dreams.

Late one Friday night, September 1964, you call and ask if I would like to go for a drive. I feel faint, my heart is racing, I am elated; what to wear? You pick me up in your white Ford convertible; it is a balmy night and the top is down. You told me how you carried my phone number in your wallet for a couple of months but didn't feel it would be good for me if you called. You knew that if you did phone and I agreed to go out with you, there would be no turning back for you, and you hoped I would feel the same. You confess to selfishly making the call anyway! Your feelings for me have become more than just those for a friend. I am speechless as well as afraid to say anything. Will you still feel the same tomorrow?

On Monday you asked me to have dinner with you on Friday; it is my birthday and our first real date; you gave me a beautiful blue crystal necklace. I didn't know you knew it was my birthday. After dinner, while driving home, you tell me that if you ask me out again and I say yes, I would also be saying yes to a marriage proposal; you don't have the time or patience for dating games; you have already wasted time dating others; and that you have had strong feelings for me for some time and knew these feelings would not change. You hoped I felt the same. What a lot to hear in one short time span; my heart was racing. I feel as if I will fall out of the car, be hit by a semi, or wake up from a wonderful dream. I am leaving tomorrow for Tennessee to visit my folks. Why now? Will you feel the same when I return? How I hate to leave you now.

You call the weekend I return and I am so anxious to see you, but when you invite me to a barbeque and to spend the day with you and the boys, I have other plans. It is Labor Day and I have made plans I can't change. I am so disappointed, I hope you will ask me again. I have forgotten what you said about the marriage proposal and frankly, had not taken you that seriously! At work the following day, you come up to me and say, "I am going to give you one more chance to say yes." That was when I realized you were serious, and I had no doubt in my mind that my answer would be yes, yes, yes! We went out again, and you made a commitment to me and I to you.

Every day at work is so wonderful; being close to you, my fear of your running off with someone else long behind me; you treat me as if there is no one else on the planet. I have never felt this way about anyone nor have I had anyone respond so openly, freely, sincerely. I can't believe my good luck. Yes, there is a God, and I believe in love at first sight or first encounter!

In the short time we are together that first night in September, I know it is the beginning of a special relationship. You believed it would eventually happen, I just hoped! We often talked about that first night and how we felt about each other, not knowing how the other felt—afraid of being hurt, disappointed. What precious time we wasted.

Our relationship began with a beautiful friendship that I will always cherish. You always teased me about being careful dating older men, and you always asked me on Mondays what I had done over the weekend—"Did I behave myself?" You were my big brother and protector!

I wrote "First Embrace" on August 9, 1995, in memory of the beginning of our special relationship.

First Embrace

Friday night I sit at home.
  Just another night
    To be alone.

I hear the ringing of my phone.
I know it's you—I cannot move;
My legs are made of stone.

You ask me out for a drive.
My knees are weak—I cannot speak;
And yet I feel so much alive.

The stars are twinkling up above.
And as you name them one by one;
I know I've found a special love.

You take my hand and squeeze so tight,
I feel a change I can't explain;
For friends we were before tonight.

Our first embrace and as we part;
You look at me so knowingly.
On this first night, you stole my heart.

And now that you have gone
Cherished memories give me peace.
Our love endures and lingers on.

Friday night I sit at home.
I feel your touch;
I'm not alone.

March 11, 1995

Once home and in bed, I don't remember falling asleep. I want to unplug the phone so I won't get that dreaded call saying that something terrible has happened. If there is no way to reach me, then it can't happen! I awake around 7:00 A.M. and immediately call the hospital. The nurse tells me that your temperature has dropped and you are resting comfortably. I am so relieved.

When I eagerly return to the hospital, with newfound hope, I see dark circles around your eyes. I have a lump in my throat, and my heart hurts for you, for us, because I know things are worse, not better. If only I had stayed with you throughout the night! Your condition grows worse each minute; you don't want to worry the boys and ask that they not come to the hospital. You just don't want them to see you like this. Why didn't someone call me? Why did I leave you last night?

Many times throughout the morning, you look at me and say, "I'm not going to make it," and I don't have it in my heart to say, "Yes, you are." I feel your pain and such sadness. You once told me you were not afraid of dying. The only thing you dreaded was not being able to be with me. Today, you tell me you are scared; how can I help you when I am scared, too?

By early afternoon you are moved to ICU and a pulmonary specialist is called in; the news is not good—you now have pneumonia. They tell me my time would be best spent at home making phone calls to the family while they make you comfortable. Reluctantly, I again leave you, hoping against hope that this nightmare will just as abruptly end. I will return. You will be sitting up with a smile on your face. You just need time to rest.

Once I am home, I keep thinking, *This is the worst day of my life.* Can there possibly be so many "worst days" of one's life? I make phone calls to the boys and ask them to call your mother and then meet me at the hospital. I then call your sister and tell her to come if she can. She calls back almost immediately and says she is on her way to the airport and will be here as soon as possible.

Again, I return to the hospital; it is 5:30 P.M. and I am not allowed to see you. I need to let you know I am here and I will not leave you again. At 7:00 P.M. I am finally allowed in your room. You are heavily sedated. However, the nurse assures me you can hear me and will remember bits and pieces of our conversation when you awaken. She tells me you know I am here; I hope you do.

As I stand here holding your hand and watching the monitor, I begin remembering all the good times we have had. They seem so long ago, and I feel so tired. Where have all those years gone and how fast! If only I could make you understand that I am here for you and that whatever you decide to do, I will accept. I want to tell you to fight with all your strength and come out of this. I also want to tell you it is okay to let go because I know you are tired and have struggled for so long; it looks like a transplant is out of the question.

You have no immune system to fight off any infections. You will be heartbroken.

How I long to turn the clock back and relive some of our "golden years"! We had some up years and some down years. I believe you have to experience bad times to balance out the good times, creating a stronger bonding as a result. We certainly were not "Ozzie and Harriet" or "June and Ward Cleaver." Maybe we were more a mixture of "The Honeymooners" and the "Flintstones"!! But we always cared for one another and each year brought us closer. We always found enjoyment in the little things we shared—the unexpected, the unusual.

Do you remember our game of hide-and-seek? I'm not sure how it got started. We had been married about one year, raising a family, with little money to go out for dinner or a movie, so we created our own entertainment.

We would shed all our clothes, turn off the lights, and close the blinds in the living room. It was so dark you couldn't see your hand in front of your face. We took turns hiding—all bedrooms were out-of-bounds so we wouldn't wake the boys. You really had to use your imagination to find places to hide. It was strangely quiet and eerie. Your heart would beat so hard and fast you could hear it, and you were sure the other person could too. You would breathlessly wait for that hand to come from out of the dark and touch you. We hid in sinks, on top of furniture, under the cushions on the couch, under the dining room table stretched across the chairs.

We often scared each other, the one seeking startled when suddenly touching the other person unexpectedly. I remember reaching around a corner to find my bearings and accidentally touched your shoulder. We both screamed. How funny to hear a grown man scream!

This was so much a part of what we were about that I had to write about our escapades in "The Night before Saturday."

The Night before Saturday

'Twas the night before Saturday, when all through the house
Not a noise could be heard, not even the breath of a spouse.
The doors were all closed and the shades pulled with care
In hopes that our bodies would soon be all bare.
The children were bathed and tucked in their beds.
While Ma and Pa, their clothes they did shed.
Your turn to hide and me, I shall not peek
As we start our weekly game of the night before Saturday
    hide-and-seek.
When out in the kitchen I stop for a drink.
There suddenly I did spy your rear perched atop the sink.
Away to the living room I flew like a flash
While giggling and exclaiming "I spy your little ass!"
The moon through the window gave such an eerie glow
We look like tree limbs, our shadows scurrying to and fro.
When what to my astonished ears I did hear,
Your footsteps coming closer, I feel you are near.
With a duck of my head I did move so quick
As you pass me by, so sure of my heart you hear tick.
I knew in a moment of me you surely must see
Alas, again you pass by I feel such glee.
For here I am atop the piano just waiting for you
I cannot keep quiet, I must yell out "boo."
As I drew in my head, you did turn around
Down from the piano I came with a bound.
And I laughed when I saw you in spite of myself
You said I looked like a figurine perched upon a shelf.
But I heard you exclaim as we scurried off to bed,
"Happy night before Saturday to all and to you I'm glad to
    be wed."

    Standing here next to you, it is so quiet. The only sound I hear is the beating of my heart and the sound of the monitor that tells me you are still with me. If only it could tell me your thoughts, your plans. There is so much I want to tell you; I know you did not want to be kept alive by machines, and I wanted to explain that these were only temporary, they were just to make you more comfortable until you could fight on your own. I feel I am once again in the dark, searching for you; please don't go.

As I look out the window, it is so black out but I do see flashes of lightning now and then. It has stopped raining and is rather pleasant outside for March. Your mother is talking to you about taking another cruise. Memories of our last one and all you have suffered take me back in time.

May 1993

We are on a cruise of the Panama Canal, a trip you have wanted to take for years. It is day four of a 17-day cruise, one day short of our 28th wedding anniversary, and one day short of going through the canal. We have signed up for a tour of the battle grounds and sightseeing in Cartagena, Colombia. It is a terribly hot day as we climb up a steep slope to view the battle grounds. Once back on the bus, you experience pain in your shoulder and can't get comfortable. We decided to cut the tour short and take a cab back to the ship. You said you just needed to lie down and would be fine once you cooled off; we were sure it was just the heat. Everyone on the tour complained about the intense heat and several people had become sick. I convinced you to let me call the ship's doctor because you were still in pain. The nurse came to our room with a wheelchair to take you to the doctor; after an EKG he told us you had experienced a mild heart attack and would have to be hospitalized.

You and I disembarked in Cartagena, Colombia, where we spent six days in the Cartagena Naval Hospital. Again, I thought these were the worst days of our lives. Not being able to speak the language, and not sure of the treatment you were receiving, not able to call home—all became an indescribable horror. I was allowed to stay in a room at the hospital; you were in ICU for three days, hooked to a monitor. On Sunday you were moved into the room with me, and I felt a bit of relief to have you near me again. You told me how concerned you were for me; you knew you would be all right, but you were not sure if I could cope. You were always so unselfish, always worrying about me.

We came through that horrible experience together and returned home safely. You were thoroughly checked by a cardiologist, and, after a couple of weeks' recuperation, returned to work. We resumed our daily routine and put the experience behind us, hoping one day to return to the Caribbean and go through the canal.

Now, here we are again, another time, another place, another hospital. Although I speak the language and know you are getting excellent care, it is again the worst day of my life. How can I help you, how often can we overcome these life-threatening obstacles?

March 1995

Wasn't it just yesterday we received the terrible news of your kidney failure?

It is Easter weekend 1994 and your kidney disease has returned and dialysis is a must. You are admitted to the hospital to have surgery to place a shunt in your arm for dialysis. Again, I feel your pain and wish there were some way I could take your place. You have been through so much in one lifetime.

I pray we will get past this. People do live with dialysis and successful kidney transplants take place daily. Now we must begin researching our possibilities for a kidney transplant. When the surgeon suggested it could be a family member or non-blood-related person, I immediately asked to be tested.

My first blood was drawn that very afternoon, starting me on a long difficult series of testing. Our sons were temporarily eliminated one-by-one and I was still being tested. I remember the day I got the first critical phone call that I was a match; I had been told prior to testing that my chances for winning the lottery were greater than becoming your match. I was elated and scared. I immediately called to tell you the news. How happy you will be. RoseMarie, a dear friend of mine, told me that when she heard I was being tested, there was no doubt in her mind that I would be a match. It just couldn't go any other way, she said, it had to be.

That night we sat in our spa and discussed surgery and our future. You expressed your concern for me having surgery. I told you that this time the decision was mine and the boys', and there would be no discussion as to whether I would have surgery. We could discuss anything else except I was going to be the donor. You always put me first, now it was your turn.

I think you knew in your heart that it was the right thing and only thing for me to do. I would have given you both kidneys if needed and without question. The boys felt the same because our love for you was so strong and we desperately wanted to hold on to you as long as possible.

After many frustrating delays and long tedious months of testing, we were finally given a surgery date of March 29, 1995. I felt I held the world in my hands. We would join those many fortunate individuals who had successful transplants and lived happily ever after.

What a long hard road we have all traveled and you have suffered all the pain. When you had your heart attack back in Cartagena, I told God that it wasn't fair that you had to suffer so much. If He was going to give you the kidney disease, the least He could do was give me the heart attack. We both suffer either way, so what difference would it make who had what.

How did you become so weak, so vulnerable? I feel so helpless standing here beside you. There is nothing I can do; it is up to you now and I fear the decision you will soon make. All of a sudden your eyes open, but you don't appear to be looking at anything. I have such a sinking feeling. When I questioned the nurse, she gently closed your eyes and said that she would put drops in to keep them from drying out if you opened them again. I thought maybe you had opened them looking for me. What did you need to see? What did you see?

As I place my hand on your chest, it is so still. The nurse said this was the quietest she has seen you all evening. It is 7:45 and I know the next shift is due at 8:00. I dread leaving you again so soon. I pray they will let me stay; we have been apart too long and each moment is so precious. What is happening? The nurse is pulling me away from you and telling us to hurry out of your room. Dear God, don't let this be the end.

Again, I am in the waiting room, away from you. Not knowing what is happening, what they are doing. Do you need me? It has been forty-five minutes and I cannot bear another minute not knowing what is happening. The nurse is headed my way—I wish I could just fade away. I can't look, and I won't listen. "We did everything we possibly could," she is saying. Dear God, why did you take my friend, my husband, my children's father, a grandfather? I must wake up; I will sit here until someone tells me they made a mistake. I can take you home now.

Death, something I knew so little about until now, affects all of us at one time or another, and has such an enormous impact upon our hearts and souls. And yet, it as been described as a beautiful and peaceful occurrence, one some anxiously await; and the beginning of a more wonderful and fulfilling life yet to be experienced.

When I was told of your death, part of me wasn't surprised. It seemed we had been delaying the inevitable for some time. Always beating the odds, it had to end sometime. However, another part of me felt as if I were living someone else's life. This could not have happened, it wasn't supposed to be like this; we were two weeks from the kidney transplant and a new life. Thus, began my struggle with two people, self-against-self, the one who believed and the one who didn't want to believe; the one who knew you were in a better place, and the one who couldn't find you.

Entering your room with the boys, family members, and friends who had come to the hospital, I find it is so dark and quiet now that the machines are gone, the lights are dimmed. You look different to me. I'm not sure what I expected. I had often heard people say how peaceful, free of pain one looks in death. I can't say I see either. I will come back, alone, to check on you, to make sure.

As I stand here with you now, alone, I keep hoping you will open your eyes; this is all a mistake. I will wake up from a bad dream. Once again I touch your face, feel for a heart beat, hold your hand; there is no feeling there for me—you have gone. But can I ever let you go? The last time we talked was 2:00 P.M. in the elevator to ICU. It is now 9:00; I already miss you.

When the nurse asked what mortuary I wanted the body sent to, I still couldn't believe this had happened and it was too soon to do anything—what if it was a mistake, what if? You were now just a "body." Why couldn't she say, "your husband," or "Wally," or "Mr. Woehler?" How cold and unfeeling life has become. I told her I would call back later.

It is very hard to leave the hospital, to leave you there all alone; yet part of me feels that if I leave it will soon be over. I will wake up to find it is a mistake. The thought of never seeing you again is something I imagine and talk about but until it actually happens, I just can't comprehend the impact it will have. We leave the hospital to go back to the house, each one following behind the other. Robert is driving me home and we are in front of the others—in our "caravan." As we drive around the corner from the hospital and head up the street, a streak of lightning lights the sky. I say to my son, "He has arrived."

I was always afraid of lightning and thunder and you teased me unmercifully when you could. You loved to sit and watch the lightning. It is a surprise to see it tonight yet a comfort to realize I am already being reminded of you by something you loved.

From the night of your death and until your ashes were scattered, I have experienced events of lightning and thunder—I wrote "Sky Show," in honor of one of God's creations that you loved so much and I had feared!

Sky Show

The night is quiet except for distant rumbling
    in the sky. Is God bowling? One
        would ask. Or is it a message
            to this mortal soul?

As it becomes closer, louder, the intensity
    of earth and sky splitting apart.
"Join me outside," you say. "It promises
    to be a spectacular sky show."

Alas, I cannot step outside. I stand
cowering as you laugh and cajole.
    "Come on out," again you say;
        "it will not bite."

As we drive home that dreary night, lights
    are all I see from our caravan. A sudden
    flash appears before our eyes. The sky
        is all aglow for one brief show.

As I watch in awe and pride,
I calmly turn to family
    and friends and softly reply,
        "He has arrived."

No more cowering in doors or under beds.
    For when I see the lightning and hear
    the thunder, I will stop and take note for
        now I know what has occurred.

It may be God bowling up above.
    But you, you are tugging at
my heart and soul. I feel your gentle
    nudge and see your smile.

How beautiful this miracle
    of His as I wait
    impatiently for the next.
        "sky show."

March 12, 1995

While trying to settle down to sleep my first night in my life without you, I felt a gentle breeze across my face. It softly, ever so tenderly, blew my hair across my eyes. The windows were closed. *Where was the breeze coming from?* I wondered as I drifted off to a peaceful sleep. Were you with me last night, kneeling beside me, watching over me as I slept; forever my protector in life, now in death? Was that your breath upon my face?

I awoke not fully aware of what had happened. Had I slept; had I dreamed; had I cried; what would I do today? This would be the first day of the rest of my life. Another "worst day."

Dr. Hardebeck, our family doctor of twenty years, called to express his condolences and assured me you had received excellent care. Dr. Spilkin, the nephrologist, also called; he was on vacation and after hearing of your death, returned to the hospital to check all the tests and procedures that had been done and also assured me that you had been given the best care possible. I still cried.

Mother, Trish, and Teresa came to spend some time with me; I just want to scream. Why can't they fix my pain, my agony? How much pain can I endure and still be there for my children?

The kids came over to help make phone calls; so many people to be contacted. I couldn't have made it through that first day without all the support and love I received. Throughout this ordeal, the boys have been there for me, with me. Even though they were in pain with their grief, they put me first and made sure I was okay just as you, Wally, had always done.

So many cards, flowers, phone calls had started to pour in—friends, neighbors were stopping by. There is an incredible amount of love all around us; sincere and unconditional. I was stunned by how many people your life had touched. I could only follow my heart now and prepare for an important time in our lives—yours, mine, the children.

I guess events that followed would best be described as a "domino effect." Once Wally died the first domino had fallen and the rest followed suit—no hesitations. Everything you do is just one more way of admitting the reality of death; of saying "yes, he is gone" when all you want to do is wake up from a horrible nightmare. You think, If I don't do this or that, everything will return to normal. I will wake up, this was a dream.

March 13, 1995

Taking that first step to the mortuary, preparing for our farewell, was very difficult. I felt that each step I took would be admitting he had died, acceptance. That was the last thing I wanted to do. The director was very nice and helpful, not at all like the horror stories you hear and read about. We actually had some humorous moments—while passing clothing from son-to-son to give to the director, the boys looked to see if there was some piece of clothing they deemed too good to be thrown away! I said you had first dibs!

Did I mention the mortuary was "Goodbody's" and the minister was "Reverend Jolly"? We got a chuckle out of that and were sure you did too. You would have been proud of how well we coped, that we went as a family, and that we were able to find some humor in the experience.

I wasn't sure of the protocol for clothing, but I knew you would want to be dressed! You always wore a dark blue suit for special occasions; without question this was to be one of those times. While selecting which suit to take with me, I pictured you on our wedding day, standing at the altar in a dark blue suit.

May 7, 1965

Preparing for my wedding day, I had lost track of the time and, when my sister and brother-in-law came in to pick me up to take me to the church, I was still getting dressed. However, I did get to the church on time. I tended to daydream and lose track of time and events.

I remember, during our single days, you once came in the office complaining about a hole in your pocket. One of the secretaries stapled it for you! Standing there at the altar, I hoped this wasn't the same pair of blue trousers! On another occasion you walked past my desk and when I looked up, I noticed a scorched impression of an iron on the back of your once-upon-a-time white shirt. Thank goodness you didn't have to take off your jacket during the ceremony! Heaven knows what might have been on the back of that shirt.

Since my father was officiating, my brother Ned gave me away. I think he was more nervous than I; prior to walking down the aisle, he kept repeating, "Don't be nervous." I wasn't until then. When my father started asking me to repeat after him, I lost my train of thought and became very nervous. I couldn't remember what he had said that I was supposed to repeat and when I looked up at him pleadingly, he very quietly repeated his last words to me. I'm not sure they made complete sentences, but I repeated them even more quietly than he so no one could hear what I was saying or not saying. You weren't sure what was happening but gave me that little nudge/squeeze—to this day I'm not sure what it was! Maybe your way of saying, "Pay attention."

You often recalled our ceremony by jokingly saying that my

father and I forgot the words and therefore the ceremony was illegal! I often recalled your blue suit and scorched shirt!

I wrote "Suit of Blue" August 11, 1995, to commemorate the beginning and the end of our life together.

Suit of Blue

This is our special day
To say our vows and pledge our troth
On this the seventh of May.

The long-awaited walk I start
As the wedding march begins to play.
It's time to join the one I've pledged my heart.

As I stand here all in white
My dreams within my reach;
I know I've found my shining knight.

When saying my vows I begin to sway.
I stutter, I stammer, I cannot speak.
A nudge from you, I remember "honor and obey."

And there you stand in your suit of blue.
So tall, so handsome, so full of wisdom;
You promise to me you will be true.

Our life of thirty years was one so rare.
Filled with joy we so lovingly shared.
On this your final day, to find peace is my prayer.

And now above me hangs a cloud.
My dress of white exchanged for black;
Your suit of blue becomes your shroud.

March 15, 1995

The house is really buzzing this morning. Jimmy and Penny arrived from Las Vegas on Tuesday and spent the night with me; they will stay for the open house on Saturday. How lucky we are to have such dear friends. Barbara and Gladys have arrived to set up the buffet and be here to greet family after the service. Your office staff has all been very helpful. They sent such beautiful flowers and plants and made donations in your name to the City of Hope. They loved you and will miss you too.

I know you always said that you didn't want a church service; you only wanted a party at the house where everyone could be relaxed, visit, and talk about the good times that were shared. Forgive me, but today we compromise, and I know you will understand; today is for me and the family. I think we need this closeness and closure. We will keep it simple.

You and I had discussed funerals we attended and how the ministers, for the most part, do not know the deceased and therefore rely upon information from family and friends. I don't want this to be an "unfeeling" service or one put together by a stranger. I met with the minister and gave him letters/notes to read that were written to you and about you by the family. I asked for some of your favorite songs; however, the pianist couldn't find her sheet music for *Rhapsody in Blue,* so she substituted with another classical; I was disappointed.

The chapel is filled with beautiful flowers from friends, family, and colleagues. As I place a yellow rose on the altar, I look at the picture taken on our wedding day and wonder when and where we will meet again. Was this just a temporary stop along the way to a more important place, a greater destiny? I feel you near me and know you are here with us today. Today is my father's birthday; your death was on your mother's—how ironic.

March 18, 1995

The ceremony on Wednesday was very special. The minister conducted the service with such warmth and compassion. He read our letters while the pianist softly played "Wind beneath My Wings."

Well, it is time to once again greet family and friends; this one's for you. We are having an open house and invitations went out to all employees. The weather is a little cloudy, but I expect it will stay on the cool side; no rain in sight. Your office is providing the food, and once again, Barbara and Gladys are here setting up.

Teresa and Debbee drove down last night to "man" the kitchen for me today. They took me out this morning for some "quiet time" and breakfast. When we returned family and friends were hard at work outside, setting up tables and chairs, moving furniture and placing the flowers and plants outside. The yard is beautiful. I know today will be just what you wanted.

Well, as another event has ended, I keep wondering where I will fit into the scheme of things when all is said and done. We had over a hundred friends, colleagues, and family come by to pay their respects. I had the kids wear name tags, as did I, because I knew there would be people coming by who would not know them, and their friends and coworkers who would not know me. You know how they reacted to that suggestion! Martha told them to humor me for a while. Before the evening was over, they had switched name tags with one another. As I watched them, I know you would have been so proud. I remember when I first met the boys and especially the day we returned from our honeymoon. Do you remember?

Mother's Day 1965

How appropriate for it to be Mother's Day on the day we returned from our honeymoon. We were married on May 7 only because the chapel was available that day. We had not picked that date for any other reason. I remember walking in the front door and the boys were standing there to greet us. I was not a complete stranger to them, having spent a lot of time with them prior to our marriage; you had wanted me to be with them on their bad days as well as their good ones. You said that would give me an opportunity to back out if I needed to and that you would understand. Well, I am still here and this will be the official day to be "Mom."

I don't recall giving my new role much thought and you just stepped aside and allowed me to take over. Having grown up with three younger brothers and sisters, many younger cousins, and done baby-sitting throughout high school—it just seemed natural, most of the time. We started off with Chris and Bobby recovering from chicken pox. Mike came down with it on Easter, and counting the incubation time, we figured Chris and Bobby would have it about the time of the wedding. Sure enough, we had to look for a sitter for them and actually ended up with someone who was a friend of a friend, of a friend!

I often said a silent thank you to Pat for entrusting the boys to my care. I believe we are placed here for specific roles and mine was to care solely for you, Mike, Chris, and Bobby after the death of Pat and Michele; that was to be my assignment. And now, I shall care for them in both of your absences and love them even more. I wrote "Mother's Day" to commemorate that special day in 1965.

Mother's Day

M is for Mother—a very special gal.
Someone we love and respect;
Who always greets us with a smile.

O is for Ours—no one more dear
Than the one we call Mom;
Who for us wipes away each tear.

T is for Timing—for which I can vouch.
For upon return from our honeymoon
There sat three wee ones upon the couch.

H is for "Honey—I'd like you to met
Mike, Chris, and Bobby who forever
will be under your feet."

E is for Enlighten—for me they did care;
For I was a new mom who had not a clue;
Just what is a mom supposed to wear!

> *R* is for Reality—how fast it does appear.
> When in the early hours of morn;
> "Can we get up now?" is the cry you hear.
>
> *MOTHER*—What a special name to hear.
> To have received that day of days;
> A family to cherish and hold near.
>
> Thank you, Wally, my best friend;
> For the trust and faith you had in me.
> For you these precious gifts till death I shall attend.

March 19, 1995

Family, friends, and overnight guests have gone, and I am alone for the first time in my life. Realization is slowly setting in; I just can't believe this has happened, that it has already been a week. I am desperately lonely for you. What could possibly motivate me to pick up the pieces, to go on living? Nothing, absolutely nothing! I lived my life for you and the boys; how can I possibly take care of myself, make myself eat, get out of bed? This is the "worst day" of my life. I can't stop the tears and this feeling of desperation. I will need help, but from where? I have never felt so alone and desperate.

Before Teresa left this morning, she told me she was taking Sara to Disney World in May and for me to think about going with her. When she asked, I felt I would suffocate. I couldn't breathe. My first thought was how could I possibly go and leave . . . leave what? I told her I would think about it; May is a long way off. I couldn't think of leaving at this time. How could I ever leave—I would not think about it now. I have never taken a trip without you; how could I do that now? I feel so numb, as if I had had surgery and my heart has been removed.

During my first fifteen minutes of "denial," the door bell rang. Chris was standing there with clothes in hand. The relationship he was in had ended and he needed a place to stay. I would have never asked any of the boys to move in with me because we all need to deal in our own ways with our change, your death. However, this no doubt has saved my life for the time being and I once again have someone to take care of other than myself. Just when I cry out for help, it is delivered. I can go on again for a little while.

How did I make it through this first week? All the planning that had to be done, greeting people, making phone calls, and just keeping it together. Everything is a blur, but I seemed to be fine. Where is that strength now—would I be lost forever?

I read in a book, Good Grief, *by Granger E. Westberg: "God has so made us that we can somehow bear pain and sorrow and even tragedy. However, when the sorrow is overwhelming, we are sometimes temporarily anesthetized in response to a tragic experience." This was true for me. I was able to function and make logical decisions most of the time put together a wonderful service and open house for family and friends. However, this was to be a temporary condition.*

March 20, 1995

I talked to the director at the mortuary today. I guess it would be appropriate to say he called to tell me your ashes were ready for pickup. But do I say I am going to pick you up, or do I say to pick up your remains, or to pick up your ashes? Tears again!

As Chris and I get in the car to return to the mortuary, it has started to rain really hard; it is cold and windy. The bleakness of the weather matches the turmoil within my heart. The director hands me a small blue bag and an envelope. I don't know which hurt more, being handed the "box" or the little envelope containing your wedding band. I am given a paper to sign—it is such an official document telling me what I must do as your caretaker. I feel like I am disposing of toxic waste. I don't know what all the fuss is about these days for disposing of remains. I have heard of ashes being scattered in back yards, gardens, etc. I know you don't really care what happens now, but it is very important for us mortals.

What an unassuming little box I hold in my hands on our way home. This is not how I wanted to take you home again. Once home, I carefully place you on the dresser in the bedroom, or should I put you in a drawer; how about the closet, or do I put "it" on display for all to view? Is there a right and wrong? I know you are laughing at me as I carry you back and forth.

I feel like an interior decorator who is moving a lamp from pillar to post, looking for that perfect niche. I don't know if anyone else would feel uncomfortable around the "box." People can be so strange at times like this. I will keep you quietly tucked away in the bedroom for now. I cannot take you to the lake until June, so I will have you with me until then. Can I take you outside to sit with me when the weather gets warm? You always enjoyed sitting on the patio. Do I place you in a chair, or on the table? Is this crazy or what? I just don't know how I am supposed to react, feel, care for you. More tears! What am I going to do with you in this box?

I am sleeping less, eating less, and not caring about anything most of the time. Each time I step outside of the house, anxiety sets in; I sometimes feel as if my heart is pounding in my throat, that my heart will explode. Returning home I become calm and feel safe and secure. What is this, and how long will this last? I feel I am on "sinking sand" and must find that "solid rock" soon.

I don't feel like talking to anyone, especially my family. Every time my mother calls, we start crying and we have to hang up. She is taking this very hard also. I just can't get past my grief. One evening my dad called to see how I was doing; I heard myself telling him that I needed time to find out who I was. My life had been turned upside down. I had never lived alone. I was always either the daughter, the wife, or the mother. Now I was just . . . I didn't know what. I realized at that time, I actually did not know who I was and that was one of the problems I had been struggling with, my new identity. Until I could reach down inside of me, I couldn't reach out to those who loved me most.

I think it is hard to relate to those closest to you (parents especially). You aren't the same person as before, the one they just talked to the day before. If you don't know who you are, how can you explain it to them? It must be a little bit like having amnesia. I don't know who I am and I am truly terrified.

The following was written on a condolence card, an outlook that I tried hard to accept:

*How beautiful, how precious is the peace that we can find
In the legacy of memories our loved ones leave behind.*

*In your memories may you find comfort.
In your friends and family may you find love.
And in your heart may you find the strength to help you
through this sorrowful time.*

I had the memories, but not the peace or comfort; I had the love of my family and friends but not the strength I needed. Where do I find these things and will I ever?

I left the house occasionally, sometimes to go for a drive with no particular destination, or walk the malls where I would be around people who didn't know the burden I was carrying. But, I was always anxious to return home. There was an incredible force drawing me back home each time. I would get such a sharp pain in my chest that I was sure I was having a heart attack except the pain seemed to be around the heart; more like a heart ache. Nothing like I had ever experienced before. I felt I must rush home to "something."

Marissa came over this evening. She said she wanted to "cook dinner for me." While dinner was cooking, we watched *Cinderella*. What a blessing it is to have her here. Don, Robert, and Chris also came over for dinner. Robert, Marissa, and Chris were outside on the patio just talking when all of a sudden the three of them came rushing in—it was funny watching three adults trying to get through the door at the same time; they seemed to be in a state of panic! They told me that one of the plants on the patio had moved! They were all three standing so close to it that they all saw it move; there was no breeze, no animals were about; the plant just went "swish." I said that was okay, but one of them would have to go back outside and bring the plant in because it was going home with Don. (I had received so many beautiful plants and flowers that I gave some of them to family and friends to have as a remembrance and this one was going to Don.) We laughed and believed you were there and this was just a small reminder that you were watching them, telling them to "behave."

Another evening Marissa and I were sitting outside alone on the patio and I was telling her of some of my "encounters" with you since your death. She was so relieved and said a couple of days after your death, when we were all together here for dinner, she was in the dining room alone and she felt you touch her. She was reluctant to tell anyone because she didn't think they would believe her. I told her I did and since we had not known her very long, I believed it was your way of telling her "Thank you" for being there for us and that you loved her.

March 25, 1995

It has been two weeks and I felt a need to return to a more normal routine, it is time to return to work. What will I do without you—we often lunched together. Who will I talk to at the end of my day? When I returned to work, I was very scared. Scared that I would fall apart, scared that I wouldn't be able to do my job, scared that my coworkers would somehow look at me differently, and mostly scared of myself. I knew the sooner I returned the easier it would be and I did need to work. Once I arrived and settled in, it was difficult to leave my desk, walk down the hallway, or even leave the building for lunch or go home at the end of the day. Now the old "anxiety" had followed me to work.

Every time the phone rings, I expect it to be you telling me you have finished dialysis and are on your way to work, or just calling to ask if I would like to have lunch. How long will this go on, the expectation of your calls?

Back at work I am in an environment that we had shared for many years. A lot of people I would run into daily, either knew you personally, knew of you, knew one of the boys, or knew me. I didn't want to have to talk to anyone; I was so tired of hearing how saddened they were by your death and I would respond with "Thank you, he was very ill." It seemed I was standing back and watching myself react. I know they all meant well, but sometimes you just want to say, "Enough!" I looked forward to the end of the day when I could retreat to the sanctity of home and familiarity.

March 30, 1995

I guess I returned to work too soon. I was unable to complete one full day all week; I will keep trying for as long as I can. Each day is getting harder and harder. Judy is so patient with me and I feel I must be letting her and my coworkers down.

I received a phone call from Payroll to come and "pick up your last paycheck." They cannot mail it to me. It has to be picked up in person. I am in so much distress—just another final act. I feel so helpless and angry that I can't even do this one small task alone; am I ever to stand on my own two feet again? How thoughtful, Nancy sensed my uneasiness and will go with me, walk that long hallway, carry some of my pain. What a true friend.

The anxiety is getting worse, making it easier to be a recluse. Getting up each day to go to work is a day of anticipation and dread. I look forward to the weekends when I can fall apart if need be, but yet dreading the lonely weekends. By Sunday I look forward to Monday when I can be around people and distracted, if for only a moment. I think of you every minute of the day and feel I will go crazy before I recover, if I recover. I fill my weekends trying to exhaust myself before bedtime.

I was never a big shopper but have found myself in the mall frequently. I would tire myself by walking from store to store; I was in a state of disarray, confusion, and completely out of focus. I know now it was good for me to force myself to go out. It would have been so easy to stay at home and slowly let my body and soul deteriorate. I needed to exhaust myself during the day so I could sleep uninterrupted at night.

April 9, 1995

I have decided to make an appointment with my doctor and see what he recommends; this can't continue. He has been our family doctor since we moved here in 1971. I trust him and know he will tell me what I need to do. Dr. Hardebeck was very kind and reassuring. He told me what a wonderful man you were and talked to me about the death of his son. He has given me a prescription for the anxiety and called my insurance for a referral for counseling. I was so relieved that he suggested counseling. I knew I could never bring it up because I always saw myself as strong, and wasn't therapy for those who had unhappy childhoods and mental problems, people always blaming their parents for their unhappiness? This wasn't me!

Without hesitation, I called and set up my first appointment. I was scared and anxious as I made that long lonely journey from the elevator to the therapist's office. Once I reached the office door, I took a deep breath and prayed my therapist would be female because I felt I would be less embarrassed when I cried; and I knew crying would be inevitable as it was already starting.

My therapist, Cyndee, was very nice and caring. She took her time and very slowly walked with me from what I perceived to be the darkest days of my life to those of almost believing that one day I would see sunshine again. She encouraged me, talked to me about the stages of grief I was experiencing, would experience, and just listened. She explained to me that I was following a normal pattern and that it *was* a hard road to travel—that I would make it back. She encouraged me to return to my normal routine as much as possible, but if I wanted to do something a little different, that was all right too.

The problem I had with all her encouragement was that I *didn't* want to make it back. All I wanted to do was get through the first couple of weeks, and I just knew God would send for me because you would tell Him you wanted me with you as badly as I needed to be with you. A small part of me was also jealous of what you might be doing and doing it without me!

I began to look forward to and feel apprehensive about my therapy sessions. Someone to talk to who wasn't emotionally involved, someone I could say anything to and not feel that I was crazy, someone with the knowledge and education to bring me through this crisis, and someone to help me once again find enjoyment in living. Yet, she could not give me the key that was to open my heart again.

I continued therapy once a week and, just as I thought I was getting well and could make it back, I had that dreaded "setback." An appointment was made with the clinic's psychiatrist. Now I really knew I was in trouble. My condition was described as "possible clinical depression" and I was told that there was medication I could take—the world-acclaimed "Prozac." I told him I didn't think I needed medication at that time and I had a doctor's appointment to see if my hormones were out of whack. If they were, that was my "clinical depression," because I am not a "depression type" of person.

Blood tests revealed my hormones were fine. The crying bouts continued and sometimes I wasn't sure I would be able to stop. Back to the psychiatrist. I decided to take his advice. It was July, I was placed on medication and now kick myself for waiting so long. After having had a talk with myself, I had to admit I couldn't do this alone and should take all the help I could get. I would now treat this as an illness and do whatever was needed to get well. However, one part of me still didn't want to get well. Thus continued my battle of self against self.

As the medication slowly took hold, I started feeling sadness rather than depression. I would still cry but not uncontrollably. The anxiety attacks have lessened in severity. However, my trips to the supermarket have become horrifying experiences. What to buy, what to cook? I can't even focus enough to know what I need. Sometimes I leave without buying anything.

As times goes on, it is becoming harder for me to relate to people. I am not interested in talking to anyone or having company. So many friends calling and offering to come and stay with me, inviting me to a movie, to lunch or dinner. The medication is helping, but I still feel out of sorts. This yo-yo condition is hard to deal with. You never know at any given moment whether you are going to be on the upswing or the downswing. I am trying to cope and take each stage as it appears and not give up hope.

Today, and every day since your death, I feel the rings upon my finger, and I have such anxiety. What do they mean now? How can I possibly take them off? Am I suppose to take them off? Would it be a sign that I am seeking another relationship? I can't deal with this tonight. I must wait for a "sign." Like every event in my life, there is a time and a place. I will not think about it tonight. I must get some sleep; I will talk to my therapist.

I asked Cyndee why my wedding rings were becoming such a painful reminder of your death, rather than a pleasant reminder of our marriage. Although she did not have the answer I was looking for, she did reassure me that as I processed my feelings over the next weeks or months, I would work through this obstacle. I think not; there have been too many obstacles to overcome and I am running out of the strength to overcome many more.

April 1995

April 11, 1995, one month after my husband's death, I had an emotional day at work and decided to sit outside once I got home. It was a warm and beautiful evening. I cut a yellow rose (our favorite), placed it on the table outside, and put on the *Phantom of the Opera* (our favorite). While I was sitting and reflecting on the last month, my neighbor's white cat came around the corner and marched up to the patio, jumped in my lap, put its head down, and purred for about three minutes. He then got up and disappeared as suddenly as he had appeared. I was dumbfounded; this cat would frequent our yard, but when he would see me through the window, he would run. He had been so skittish that I don't think you could have enticed him with a mouse! I guess he sensed my loneliness and decided to keep me company, if only briefly. How strange.

Chris and I will spend Easter weekend with Teresa. This will be my first time away from the house overnight, and I am quite anxious about leaving. When we arrived, Chris took my overnight bag out of the car and commenting on its heaviness said, "Mom, what do you have in here?" I replied, "Your dad." He and my sister looked at me, then at one another. I think they were trying to decide which one should take the responsibility to have me committed. When I saw the looks on their faces, I said, "Just kidding." I did tell them that if anyone had said to me, "Don't forget to pack Dad," I probably would have thought it was okay to take him!

I was able to be away for the weekend but was equally glad when I returned home. I did make a commitment to Teresa that I would go with her to Florida in May. It would be a birthday present from me to my grandson, Kyle. I needed to see if I could do this, and I knew I would have to be okay for Kyle's sake.

Still having trouble getting to sleep, I just can't shake these horrible feelings. Earlier I started a journal at the suggestion of friends who had lost loved ones and said they found it to be comforting to write in at night. I was willing to try anything; however, I found myself each night writing the same request; "I miss you so much, please help me deal with this."

One night, when I hadn't been able to sleep, I had reread some of the condolence cards and decided to write Wally a condolence card and forego the journal. I had ended up writing "Wally's Poem." However, I have never felt that I had written the poem but that he was communicating to me. Having never written anything before—I had no idea how important this first poem would become to me.

It was later pointed out that "Wally's Poem" was written on March 29, 1995, the day we were scheduled for our surgery. This would also be the beginning of my writing and healing process.

Wally's Poem

Come, sit here awhile with me.
Listen to the birds as they sing their melodies.
Hear my voice in the breeze,
I'll tell you why I had to leave.

No time to grieve, no time for tears.
My life was brief but filled with good years.
Friendships unforgotten, a peaceful home; I had so much.
Joy, laughter, my loved one's touch.

The path I have taken is new, you see.
No more pain, no more agony.
I heard the call. I could not stay.
I took His hand. He led the way.

It's time to go and live anew.
Another life, another view.
So good-bye and peace to thee.
We'll meet again when He comes to set you free.

I had asked donations be sent to the City of Hope in lieu of flowers but also received money to use as needed. After talking to Nancy, a coworker, I accepted her suggestion that I use the money for a memorial bench. I decided a bench at Wally's work site would be a nice memorial.

When I showed *my* poem to the boys, they were just as surprised as I had been when they read it; Chris thought his dad had written it but was confused by the date on the bottom. I told them about the money that was coming in and that I would like to have a bench dedicated in their dad's memory. It was at that time that I decided to have the poem inscribed on the bench if possible.

Harold and I found the perfect bench and could indeed have the poem inscribed without any problem. While we were sitting in the office waiting for the contract to be drawn up for signature, the desk calculator next to me started running. It was as if someone had entered a couple of figures, then pressed the total button. A portion of the tape printed out. The owner, who was drawing up the contract, looked over and asked if I had touched the calculator. At the same time, I was checking to see if my chair was on the cord or if the cord was loose. Neither was the case; Harold and I started laughing. I told the owner that Wally had been a budget analyst and was probably checking her figures. When I got home that night, I discovered she had left "Jr." off after his name. I called back and asked that it be added and since I had already paid for the bench, I would stop by and pay for the addition. After she told me there would be no charge, I said I guess Wally was trying to add in the additional cost before we left and we weren't paying attention!

May 8, 1995

Once again, friends and family have gathered in support of my request and have planned a dedication ceremony to be held on May 8, 1995, one day following what would have been our thirtieth wedding anniversary.

It is a cloudy day; very similar to the day you died. I called your office this morning to see if the bench had arrived. Velma told me it was there and that it was beautiful; while they were wiping it off, the sun came out and the birds began to sing. As soon as it was clean and covered up, awaiting the dedication, the sun retreated to hide under the clouds and the birds mysteriously disappeared as quickly as they had arrived. Velma said it was a very eerie yet a heartfelt moment. I hope it was you sending your approval.

Now the American flag is at half-mast in your honor. I am so proud. Proud to have been your wife, proud to have raised your children, and proud to see the love for you on this special day.

Just when I felt I was coming to understand the "why" of Wally's death, the "just where is he" began to give me problems. What did I believe? What did I want to believe? I was raised in a Christian environment; my father was a Baptist minister. No matter how religious I was or thought I was, all my beliefs flew out the window. I desperately wanted to talk to someone who had a sense of what I was going through. A lot of people would come up to me and say, "I know just how you feel, when my grandmother died" or when "my uncle died." I know they meant well, but how could they know what it is like to lose your spouse of thirty years, your best friend of thirty years, and your soul mate of thirty years all at once?

This became my angry stage and presented itself most often in the middle of the night. Something would have awakened me and while trying to get back to sleep, I once again tried to sort out where he was and what he was doing. It suddenly dawned on me that if I believed we would be reunited with our loved ones in another life (which I so wanted to believe), then Wally was with his "first wife," and she was only 29; what would he want with an old broad like me when I died? I became very angry. I just couldn't get things in perspective; I was in a state of confusion. Later, when I related this story to my therapist, I was able to laugh about it—but I was still angry!

Wally and I used to listen to a particular radio station and would always ask if the other heard, on the way to work, so-and-so. The disc jockeys, Joe and Mac, had been on this station for twenty years. One night, as we were watching the news on TV, they announced that Joe's wife had died suddenly. We were both saddened by this news. We had often listened to him talk about his wife and family; he was my age, and they had been married about as long as we had.

Now while listening to Joe talk on the radio about his upcoming marriage, I decided to write to him and ask how he had gotten through the death of his wife. I felt I was drowning in my sorrow. It took me a couple of days to get up the courage to mail my letter. My thought was: *What do I have to lose? I have already lost everything that meant anything to me.* My letter was answered by a phone call immediately upon receipt. Joe was very kind and talked to me about his loss and what I could/would do and how it seemed impossible at this time for me, but he promised me it would get easier in time.

When I told Joe that I had a need to know where Wally was and to have my faith restored, he recommended I read, *Embraced by the Light*, by Betty J. Eadie. That following Saturday I bought her book and spent the entire day reading. It was so uplifting for me; it gave me new hope.

A passage in her book really struck home: "Most spirits choose to remain on earth for a short time and comfort their loved ones; families are subject to much more grief than the departed one. Sometimes the spirits will remain longer if the loved ones are in despair. They remain to help the loved ones' spirits heal." This single passage answered so many of my questions and gave me such reassurance.

I know that this was true because of the many things I had experienced. At first I thought it was because it was what I wanted to believe. My husband would have helped me as much as he could and for as long as he thought necessary. In rereading my journal, on Sunday, I found that on April 23, 1995, I had written, "Somehow I haven't felt your closeness since Thursday night. Have you left me on my own?" I checked my journal for that Thursday night and I had written, among other things, "Felt a little depressed when I got home tonight, I sure miss you."

As written in "This House," I believe that was when he decided it was time to go and leave me to start dealing with my grief. However I feel at times when I am at my lowest, he returns to be here for me and will continue to do so.

This House

The shutters in this house remain closed and barred
to keep out a light. A light these dull, listless eyes
cannot bear to behold.

Eyes that looked into yours and saw fear and foreboding.
Eyes that pleaded and searched for reassurance.
Eyes that embraced for a final good-bye. Eyes that told
children their father was gone.

The doors in this house remain closed and barred to
keep me out of harm's way. How can I leave when I
feel so protected, belonging, here—in this house?

Oh, what comfort I do find each time I return to this house.
Like a butterfly returned to its cocoon, a lost child to its
mother's bosom.

I must not leave again.

I hear your voice in the dark as it softly lulls me to sleep.
I feel your embrace when I'm so alone and lost. You are
the breath I take, my heartbeat. We are one, here in this
house.

Why do I feel such anxiety and trepidation as I enter this
house today, as I go from room-to-room, searching for I
know not what? Has someone been here, an intruder, a
trespasser? What was taken from me, from this house?

It is so empty, so dark, so cold—this house. Have you
gone and left me to repair my soul? Have you started a
life anew—away from this house?

I did not know you were here until you were gone.

I must not leave again.

I always enjoyed working in the yard as well as in the house. It gave me satisfaction to see something I had planted actually take root, bloom, and grow; and to paint or wallpaper, creating a different look. But for the first few weeks I couldn't bear to go outside and nothing in the house interested me. I didn't want to work in the yard and chance running into any of my neighbors and having to talk; I had a need to keep the inside of the house looking the same as it was when we were both sharing it.

While driving around one morning, no destination in mind, I stopped at a furniture store where Wally and I had looked at furniture just weeks before his death. I decided to go in and see if they still had the couch I had liked, and if it was still there, that would be a sign to purchase it! Also, Wally had suggested that I get a cabinet for my dolls; now my trip was twofold. I did see the same couch and a cabinet I liked, but I couldn't decide which one to buy. I stood there and asked myself, *What would Wally do?* He would say, *You are here and they have what you want, the price is right, so buy them both.* So I did! I was starting to take some interest in my home once again. It was hard to make that first "change." To get rid of things we had picked out together, which would be replaced by new ones that only I had purchased. As we had been in this store together, I was able to make this change. At least he had seen the couch; whether he liked it . . . ?

I slowly began to spend more time working in the yard. First just for a minute or two, looking at my flowers; and then slowly working my way up to spending three or four hours at a time, just trying to wear myself out. It was a place where I could get hold of my feelings and have total silence to think and feel.

One morning I was trimming one of the trees when I started humming—something I hadn't done since his death. I began to think about Wally and I had this incredible sense of happiness. I just stood there and said, "I finally know who I am; I know this person Wally married and why; and most of all, I like me; I was good for him and we raised incredible children." What an insight! I stopped to smell the roses! I believed this was a turning point for me. I understood life and death better; not only the why but the how.

I expressed my newfound knowledge that fall in "Tulips." Taking life one-step-at-a-time, my ultimate goal—to finish therapy and walk on my

35

own, and to complete the cycle of grieving and know I can still love Wally but in a different yet fulfilling way. He lives again as I shall.

Tulips

Tenderly the tulip bulbs are placed in the ground,
in rich, moist soil. Covered ever so gently to be
nurtured and cared for until the arrival of spring.

Like the tulip, I nurtured and cared for you
as we too patiently awaited the arrival of spring
and for the gift of life I so lovingly would give
to you.

Spring has come, the tulips mysteriously appear
as if on cue. How beautifully they present
themselves as they show off their rainbow of colors.

Stately, whimsical tulips sway in the early
morning breeze. Their petals glistening with the
kiss of dew.

Tenderly you take my hand as once again we
face uncertainty. How brave you are as I
look into your eyes. Tears glistening on my
face like the dew upon the tulips.

Spring came and you quietly slipped away.
The gift of life unopened. I feel such pain
and defeat.

The tulips have also faded and slipped away.
Their tiny bulbs wait impatiently in the ground.
Once again to be cared for as the cycle of
life goes on and on.

May 1995

Since I had not scattered Wally's ashes, I was still apprehensive about leaving home for any length of time. A part of me felt I should stay home with him. I can see how easy it would have been to keep his ashes around. I knew he would never have forgiven me if I had. I could cherish his memories in my heart, but he needed to find peace and go on to his destination. Due to weather conditions, I would not be able to do this until June.

I had made a commitment to take my grandson to Florida. May rolled around sooner than I liked, but here we were, off for a week of fun and sun. Teresa took charge of me, Sara, and Kyle. I didn't have to make any decisions, if I wasn't up to it; and believe me it was difficult enough just to get myself dressed for the day! It was also to be the beginning of a newfound friendship. As I am older, I didn't grow up with Teresa. This would be an opportunity to get to know her and my niece.

It was good for me to be distracted by children. They have such different needs and can often take you by surprise. While standing in line for one of the rides, Sara turned to ask me where Uncle Wally's grave was. I told her I hadn't picked one out yet. She seemed satisfied with that information, and I wasn't sure the moment was appropriate to explain cremation, and I didn't want either child to visualize his ashes sitting at home on the dresser. She and Kyle then proceeded to argue over who had cried the most and who had lost more relatives, the grave site long forgotten—what a blessing to be so easily satisfied and have things so simple and innocent.

On the way back to the hotel, we encountered a bit of lightning activity in the distance—not my favorite of God's creations. We watched in awe as it appeared to be gaining on us. As it came closer, we could hear the thunder. Sara asked me if I knew what caused the lightning and thunder. Kyle was giving her the scoop on the atmospheric conditions and when he finished, she said, "Someone told me thunder was God bowling; did Uncle Wally know how to bowl?" I told her he had last bowled in high school and could possibly be bowling. Teresa whispered to me that we weren't sure he was there yet (ashes not scattered). At that moment a huge streak of lightning appeared in the sky right in front of us. It scared all four of us, it was so sudden and bright. I turned to Teresa and asked if she had any other comments, at which she replied, "Nope, that about covers it." I guess he was there.

I am glad I found the strength to pull myself together to take this trip. It enriched me in so many ways; I found I could do things on my own, I was in control of my life, and I had found a new friend. I knew I would need to push myself to do things, if I was to ever get well.

Sometimes we have to try new experiences in order to remake our lives. It is true that your life will never be the same and you have to find the road back to a meaningful life. I felt that I was truly on my way back; little did I know the road back was longer and bumpier than I ever imagined. This was just a very, very tiny part of the healing process. But nonetheless, a part of me was healing.

June 1, 1995

June is here and I am having second thoughts of taking you so far from home, from me. However, as I continue to make my plans, I hope something/someone will intervene. I just don't want you so far away. Am I being selfish? I don't know when I decided to take you back to Michigan. You had so often talked about the great times you had had, as a young boy, with your cousins on a lake there and how much you wanted to go back with me for a vacation. How ironic, I am making plans to take you back to find your final resting place—somewhere I have never seen. How can I do this? Is this what you want?

June 5, 1995

Chris and I left for Wisconsin with a stopover in Las Vegas where we spent a couple of days with Jimmy and Penny and picked up your sister who would accompany us to Michigan. I felt I was on a journey that would never end, but all I had to say was "No, I can't do this," and we would be on our way back home. But, I still felt in my heart it was the right decision.

June 7, 1995

We arrived in Wisconsin where we spent the night with your cousin Richard and his wife, Mimi. I could see why you had such fond memories; Richard and Mimi were unbelievably warm, loving, and caring. The following morning we left for the lake house in Michigan. We made a detour through Oak Park where you were born and lived for several years. It was a beautiful tree-lined street. As we stared out the car window, I could visualize you riding your bike up and down the sidewalk. It was just as you had described. It was so meaningful to me to take this trip with you; to see where you were born and to lovingly leave you in your final resting place.

You often talked to me about living in Oak Park as a small boy, and I would tell you about growing up in Covington. We discovered our paths could have crossed so many years ago.

April 1958

I was a freshman in high school in Covington, Tennessee (just outside of Memphis). My father was the minister at a small church in nearby Millington. You were in the Navy and had a brief stay in Memphis. You said you and your buddies often went to Millington some weekends. I was so shocked; our paths could have crossed. I know you wouldn't have given me a second glance, had we passed on the street. I was fifteen, skinny, freckle-faced; you were twenty-three, tall and handsome in your uniform. Thank goodness our paths never crossed.

June 8, 1995

We arrived at the lake house late afternoon. What a beautiful place. I can see why you loved it here and had so much fun as a young boy. Yes, I have made the right choice. I feel such relief. Tonight, as I lie in bed, I wonder what will I do tomorrow, how will I feel after I leave you, where will you be? I still need answers.

Saturday morning, we are the only ones on the lake; how

beautiful and calm. As I unwrap this "little box"—is this another farewell? I ask myself as I hold you one last time. The tearing of the paper that encases your box emulates the tearing of my heart. I know I must let you go.

> Beneath His wings of love abide,
> God will take care of you.
> Lean, weary one, upon His breast,
> God will take care of you.

My work is done and on June 9, 1995, you and I crossed a lake hand-in-hand to embrace eternal peace.

I awoke the next morning to a light rainfall. While I was gazing across the lake, a streak of lightning lit up the sky. Chris turned to me and said, "Why not? lightning has been present in all our events surrounding Dad's death." Again, is this your way of getting my attention, to tell me you are home and now I must return? Once again I felt the reality of my loss, for now I believed I had nothing. How could I possibly keep going? I had made it this far, hard as it has been, but I have no strength left.

"Last Farewell" was the hardest for me to relive and capture on paper. That day was the hardest day I have ever had in my life and was more painful than the day he died. I was forced to accept his death as his ashes slowly drifted away from me.

Last Farewell

I stand here and gaze upon the lake.
A lake where you played as a young boy.
A lake that will embrace you now as you find
your final resting place. What force has drawn
me here, to this lake?

It is so calm, so quiet, so mesmerizing. The
silence is broken from rustling of paper that
enshrines this "box." Such an unassuming
"box" I hold with trembling hands. A lifetime
of living, loving, caring, pain, and suffering.
How did this come to be?

I gently lift the lid and let your ashes flow.
Drifting, lingering, slowly sinking below.
As the deed is done, I see a sparkle in the
water. Millions of stars twinkling like gold.
Or is it tears in my eyes clouding my view?

As I turn back for one last farewell, ripples
upon the water are like footprints upon the
sand, escorting us back to shore. Are you
following, our last moment together, your
last farewell?

As I stand here on the balcony looking upon
the lake; why did I bring you so far from home?
Will I ever return and when I do will it be to
join you?

I turn to leave, to make that long, lonely journey
home. To what awaits me I know not.
Lightning and thunder fill the sky above. Is
this is your way of telling me, "Good-bye, job well
done"?

So many questions run through my mind.

June 12, 1995

It is my first day back at work and when I returned from lunch, I was given a phone message that my brother-in-law had died. The message wasn't clear and I was thinking he was in his late 60s or early 70s, he and my sister Pat had been divorced for some time, and he had moved to Oregon. While all this was going through my mind, I heard the message being repeated, "Your brother-in-law in St. Louis." I said that couldn't be right because my brother-in-law lived in Oregon. It suddenly hit me that it was my other brother-in-law, Don, Teresa's husband, Sara's father, they were talking about. Don was only fifty, what could have happened? I was, once again, in shock. I just couldn't believe death was once again at our door. I felt numb, disoriented. Wally was the only one dead. I had just returned from Michigan, hadn't I? Someone was confused. Who was playing this cruel joke?

I immediately called to talk to Teresa; yes, Don had died of a heart attack. She was devastated. Even though she and Don were divorced, they had maintained a good relationship. He was always there for her and Sara when they needed him. Sara had just arrived in St. Louis to spend time with her dad and was with him when he died. What could that little one be going through all alone and so far from home?

As Teresa talked to me about her concern for Sara, who was in a strange place, staying with strangers, and her mother couldn't get a flight out to St. Louis until morning, my heart hurt for them, a mother who couldn't get to a daughter who desperately needed her and a little girl who had just witnessed the death of her father and needed her mother. I told her I would go with her and bring Sara back or stay there with them, whatever was needed. I had suddenly regained my strength and knew I now had to be there for them as they had been for me and my family. My sorrow and grief were put on hold.

After Teresa returned from St. Louis, we talked frequently. I started recommending books for her to read that had helped me. Once again, we all have different needs when we face such a tragedy. However, I prayed she would draw the same hope and reassurance I had; heaven knows I certainly had the experience. I was a few steps ahead of her with my grieving.

October 17, 1995, I called Sara to wish her a happy birthday. I noticed an unusual quietness and sadness in her voice, which inspired me to write "Our Fathers" for her and the other children in our family.

Our Fathers

How do you explain to a child her father has gone away?

How do you fill the void he has left behind?

How do you replace the pain you see on her face, hear in her voice, with smiles and laughter long forgotten?

Who will sit in that chair and not feel his presence?
Is it best to remain vacant?

How do you explain to grandchildren their grandfather has gone away?

Who is going to cheer you on when you play your heart out and still lose that important game?

Tell you what a beautiful young lady you have grown up to be?

Encourage you as you strive to become a man?

How do you explain to a special niece and nephew their uncle has gone away?

How can you assure them it was for the best, yet allay their anxieties for their fathers, only to stand helplessly by as fear becomes reality for one precious child?

Can we truly find comfort from the love we shared, solace in cherished memories we recall, inner peace from above, and strength to walk that long lonely path—
to what end?

How do you explain to a wife that her husband has gone away?

Is this the end of another life or just the beginning?

TODAY, the tender Leaves of hope . . .
TOMORROW, blossoms (Shakespeare)

July 1996

I bought two bedside table lamps that turn on and off by touch. I had just fallen asleep when the lamp next to my side of the bed suddenly came on. It startled me at first; I smiled, reached over to "touch" it off, and went back to sleep.

Another incident occurred when I stayed home from work with a cold and cough. I was depressed because it was the first time I had been sick and alone. While lying in bed listening to the radio, I watched the rain from my bed. It was dark in the bedroom and I had turned on the lamp. Periodically the sun would peek out and light up the room ever so briefly. All of a sudden, there was a downpour, darkness; then clearing followed immediately by sunlight. The room was so bright I looked up to see what had happened. And then, as if on cue, the bedside lamp went off. My first thought was: *Oh, well I didn't need it on anyway.* Wally was a stickler when it came to turning off unneeded lights in the house!

Last week I got home after dark and as I turned the key to unlock the door, I remembered a time when Wally and I came home late at night. He unlocked the door and opened it for me. As I stepped in the house, he said, "I shouldn't do that." When I asked what he was talking about, he said, "Open the door for you and have you go into a darkened room first. I should go in first and turn the lights on and make sure it is safe before you come in." As I prepared to enter a darkened house, I realized it wasn't as dark inside as I had expected. As I looked down the hallway, I noticed a light coming from the bedroom. I immediately knew what had happened. The lamp by the bed was on again. I just smiled and said, "Thank you."

I guess I should have the outlet checked to see if it is a shortage setting the lamp off and on; but what the heck, it's fun to think he is still around now and then watching over me. Every time the light comes on, I think of him.

It has been one of those days when everything that could go wrong has gone wrong. If you were here, we would sit and talk and everything wouldn't seem so traumatic. You have a way of putting things in perspective.

When I got in the car to go home from work, the battery was dead; and I don't know how that could have happened since the car is less than two years old. I called the Automobile Club and they were here in a flash. The next morning I couldn't get the radio to play or the CD player. When I looked in the manual, it described a safety mechanism that comes on when the battery goes dead to protect the radio from theft. I can reset this system. No problem!

As I finish step five, step six is: "Enter security code." Of course! Well, I started with your birthdate because that is what we used most of the time. Well, that didn't work! Over the course of three days, I racked my brain with numbers—my birthdate, your Social Security number, our home address, our telephone number, your work number, my work number.

I had nine choices before the system would "crash" and I would have to take it to the dealer! After eight failed attempts, I called the dealer and was told to go ahead and crash the system and then bring it in; as I sat in the car, I debated whether to try your birthdate again or another date I had not tried. I just knew it should have been your birthdate. When I got to the last step, at the last second, I punched in your birthdate. The bells and whistles went off, the radio came on, and a message that the security system was now released flashed. I just sat and laughed. I must have fumbled with the steps the first time I tried. When I told my son what had happened, he said you were just toying with me! These little things in life seem so magnified and irritating to me; you should be here to fix them.

Finding the correct code to reset the audio system haunted me for days. Instead of going to the dealer and having it corrected, I continued my search. It became a major event in my life until solved.

September 18, 1995

I did most of my writing in August and September 1995. I think that was when I was in the most turmoil, depression. The reality of your death was becoming more apparent as the days grew longer for me; struggling with my inner self and trying to maintain stability with my outer self.

On August 9, 1995, after writing "First Embrace," I decided to take important events in our life together and write them down, hopefully, in verse form. Our short dating "season" is so vivid to me to this day; it was easy to go back in time; remembering your words to me, your touch. It was an experience that I don't know that I will ever have again.

On August 11, 1995, while writing "Suit of Blue," I wasn't sure how it would end. As I was writing, words were leaping ahead of me. It is one of the shorter verses because I was so anxious to end it and get on paper what was so painful for me. I guess this was my way of expressing joy and pain in one moment of verse.

And of course, our wedding memories would not have been complete without "Mother's Day," which was written on August 21, 1995. The two most important events in my life would have to be my wedding day and the day I became a mother (threefold). Instant motherhood would be the shaping of my life, not only as a mother but as a person and a wife to you. I am so proud of the boys today that I guess we did something right.

September 19, 1995

September was to be a more difficult month; my first birthday without you since I turned twenty, your birthday, a daughter-in-law and granddaughter's birthdays. It was a month we enjoyed being outdoors. With perfect weather every day as we drifted into fall. I wrote "Saturday Night" as an event in our life that was fun and fun to remember, talk about, and share; a secret no one knew about. It was fun to write because it came together so well. I remember hiding on the piano and you hiding in the sink more than any other hiding place. Sometimes I feel as if you are still hiding from me; I keep looking.

On the Sunday before my birthday, I was working outside and fell and hit my knee against a ladder. My knee became so swollen that I went to the emergency room for treatment. I didn't feel a need to call anyone to go with me, but once I got there, the nurse was asking for health information and when she heard why I was on anti-depressant medication, she told me her husband had recently died. She began crying for "me." She said she knew what I was going through and felt so sorry. I didn't expect this; it added to my sadness, sadness for her and me.

Since yesterday was my birthday, I expected you to call and I found myself waiting for you to walk in the door. I haven't been able to think of anything except your death. How far we had come, how quickly you left, what were your thoughts those last hours I was unable to be with you, did you know when I was there with you and how much I cared? Tonight I will try once again to relieve my anguish through my writing.

Before I began my writing, I read some of the book given to me yesterday for my birthday by my good friend and colleague. Elizabeth. The book, In the Palm of Your Hand, *by Steve Kowit, is actually a lesson in writing: "To write poetry is to perform an act of homage and celebration—and this even if one's poems are full of rage, lamentation, and despair. To write poetry of a high order demands that we excise from our lives as much as we can that is petty and meretricious and that we open our hearts to the sufferings of this world, imbuing our art with as luminous and compassionate a spirit as we can. Choose an incident that calls up strong emotions and which might have had consequences for your emotional life." Based on that description, I couldn't possibly have written anything other than "The General."*

The General

I found him sitting in his favorite chair, so
quiet, so vulnerable, so much in pain. And
yet, he had a smile for me as I entered the
room.

As I lean down to kiss his forehead, I feel
intense heat radiating all around. I draw
back in fear and reluctance as I slowly walk
to the phone.

With shaking hands I make the call; I hear
the words I've come to dread.

As we drive away my thoughts come flooding
in. Will I ever bring you home again? What
are you thinking, are you as scared as I?

The roses in the yard stand so tall and majestic.
They look like soldiers on parade, their heads
softly floating with the wind, saluting as the
General passes by.

It has stopped raining; the sky is black as night.
Far off in the distance the clouds are scurrying
to-and-fro as if preparing for some special
event.

My heart is breaking piece-by-piece as we drive
farther and farther away. Away from our life,
our home, our children.
* * *
I stand here before you now. The room is so
dark and quiet; not like before. An occasional
light from the sky illuminates your room.

I kiss your forehead to say a final good-bye.
May you rest in peace and find a new home
where you wait for me.

The roses lie scattered upon the ground as
though their petals were plucked one-by-one.
Each tomorrow will bring a new rose to
stand tall, majestic, in all their splendor to
salute as the General passes overhead.

    As I became more confident in my writing, not sure that each
poem would be my last, not sure where this sudden creativity was

leading, I began sharing them with family and co-workers. I expected someone to say, "Well, this is good but not as good as the last one you wrote," or "I like this one better than the last one." Thus, giving me the excuse to stop writing. Although it was often difficult to relive the experience, I viewed my poems as release and fulfillment rather than sadness and desperation. But my co-workers read them with tears in their eyes and remarked how touching and sad they were.

When I would come in with a new one they would remark, "Oh no, not another one, where is my tissue?" Finally, after writing "Last Farewell," I realized what an impact this one could have, several of my co-workers knew Wally. I placed my poem on Susie's desk with a box of tissues. This became automatic with Susie, poem in one hand, box of tissues in the other. Susie and I frequently lunched together and talked about death. Our talks helped me understand different forms of loss and grieving as I continued to work through my feelings.

Today, when I read my poems, I cry.

September 27, 1995

Today is your birthday, and I am flooded with so many memories. Memories of our first year together as well as our last. How much I miss you and how I hate the unfairness of your death. How life takes an unexpected turn that can so quickly leave one questioning one's faith. I am listening to a CD of Elvis that I recently bought. The song now playing describes perfectly my pain and suffering tonight: "Farther Along" by W.B. Stevens.

I am trying so hard to get "farther along," to understand the meaning of your death and to restructure my life. I feel so cheated, why couldn't someone more deserving die? Some days I feel I have made progress and others I feel as if there is no point in making progress because I have no future. Recapturing our life together is helping me immensely in my process.

I wonder how the street where you lived as a young boy must have looked, trying to recreate it as I remember it from this last June as our journey took us through Oak Park. Our childhoods were so different, yet, when fate crossed our paths, we knew we were destined to walk together until we reached the end of our new path.

Tonight I have written "Celebration of Life" to picture our different childhoods, how our lives might have crossed before being destined to, and our predestined fate.

Celebration of Life

Where did it all begin?
The entwining of two souls, their long
journey down a path laden with
obstacles too painful to bear.
Was it while a young boy rode
his bike up and down a
sidewalk lined with trees?
Was it a thousand miles away where
a little girl built castles in the sand
while her mother tended the garden?
Was it years later in a small Southern
town as they passed on opposite
sides of the street?
Or was it when two young adults walked
hand-in-hand down a path that
promised imperishable love?
Where does it all end, this journey?
Does it end in a dark and lonely
hospital room where one precious
soul draws his last breath?
Or beside a lake where one life flows
gently away, freely and boundlessly as
the other stands silently crying
upon its shores?
A special life flows on forever, is never lost,
and can never pass away.
May the love of those we hold near to
our hearts sustain us and may the

celebration of life be sheltered by memories
of those we loved and who loved us in return.

October 1995

Autumn was one of our favorite times of the year. Warm, yet not hot; cool, yet not cold. It is a beautiful autumn day; the leaves on our liquidambar are turning gold. I remember when you and I purchased it; we were so excited that we could plant a tree here that would actually change colors and drop their leaves like the ones back east. You were disappointed the first couple of years because it didn't seem to be growing. But this last year it really took off and shot up toward the heavens. When you saw how beautiful, full, and colorful it had become, you called to me to bring my camera and take a picture. You said it was more beautiful than any of its kind you had ever seen.

While writing "Autumn," I was struggling with whether to use "dancer" or "ballerina" and I could not remember how to spell "pirouette." During the course of my dilemma, a song came on the radio—Nat King Cole singing "Dance, Ballerina, Dance," and as I listened (in shock/apprehension) to the lyrics, I decided to go with "graceful dancer," as I did not feel pirouette was the right choice of words after all.

Then, in the midst of my dealing with "magnificent or dazzling jewels in the trees," the Carpenters came on the radio singing a song about trees. Now, I am **very** aware/alert and somewhat anxious and calm all at the same time—anxious because it is so bizarre that every time I was stuck on a word or phrase, a song came on and cleared up the problem; calm because it feels right.

I finally finished "Autumn," the last line being "The wind blew, and you were gone." I closed my book and as I reached to turn off the radio, I heard the DJ say "and that was 'Cast Your Fate to the Wind.'" Throughout this phenomenal event, two small lights across the room kept flickering off and on.

With some apprehension, I turned off the radio and lights and settled down for a restless night's sleep.

Autumn

I watch the sun slowly drift behind these barren
hills. Reminding me another day has
ended as quickly and quietly
as it began.

I watch the sun reappear each morning as it
beckons to me. A new day is dawning;
a promise of hope and reassurance.

I hear the birds outside my window as they
awaken one by one. Greeting me
with their chatter as they
flutter from branch-to-branch.

I see the trees bending, swaying like a
graceful dancer in the autumn breeze.
Their trunks adorned with dazzling jewels
of red and gold.

Why does the night approach and fill my
heart with sorrow and yet
anticipation of a new tomorrow?

Why does the sun rise to fill this room
with glowing rays and yet I
feel no warmth?

Why does one lonely songbird sit upon my
windowsill and sing its song so
quietly as though in reverence
of your passing?

Why do we seek such pleasure in watching
nature paint its leaves with such care
and beauty only to be torn from
their branches and tossed to the wind?

> Like the seasons that come and go quickly,
> quietly; so must we. The wind
> blew and you were gone.

October 25, 1995

We had a habit of always calling one another if we were going to be late, keeping in constant touch as to one another's whereabouts. Also, since being on dialysis, you would always call me when you were finished just to let me know things went well. Sometimes people would have dizzy spells, or the artery would reopen and bleed profusely. I still wait for your call and when the phone rings, for that brief second, I wonder if it is you.

Tonight I have suddenly realized I left the phone in the other room; in a panic I hurry to retrieve it to place it by my bed. What is the rush, the panic? I am still anticipating a call from you to tell me where you are, when you will be home! Why won't you call me or why can't I call you? It seems like a simple request.

I became very angry and frustrated with the world. With all the technology, since there is supposed to be a hereafter, why can't we pick up the phone and call? For the next five minutes or so, I struggled with my "dilemma." It seemed so real to me and such a possibility that I couldn't think past trying to make that phone call. It is hard to explain my anxiety and the reality of making that phone call as I stood there with the phone clutched in my hand. After a bout of tears, I decided to try to express my concerns in my writing.

Since this was such a real possibility to me at the time, I started to laugh when I rationalized the whys and ifs. It was very easy for me to write "Heaven's Call," one of my favorites.

Heaven's Call

Hello, operator? I would like to make a long-distance phone call,
 person-to-person. Oh yes, and make that collect.

The number? 1-800-HEAVENS.

Hello, Heaven!

Who's calling? It's me, Geneva. My husband Wally was inducted
on March 11 of this year. Remember the night you sent that bolt of
lightning that scared the hell—oops, sorry.

Yes, yes, that's me!

Can I hold? Well, okay. Oh, you have "call holding" and another call
is coming in? Busy night, is it?

What department is Wally in? Well, I don't know. Don't you have
an Information Desk?

Oh, sorry—no one in that capacity has died? No, no, I'm just a
secretary.

Try your Budget Department. I'm sure you have one, don't you?

Hello, Heaven's Budget Department? May I speak to Wally?

Oh, he's not there right now? Well, where is he?

I see, he's at the World Series. Yes, yes, I'm sure he has important
work to do. I wouldn't call if—I know, but. You'll take a
message? Thanks, tell him his wife called.

Which one?

Yes, you do have a sense of humor, sort of!

Please, just have him call me when he returns.

Does he have my number? Oh, God—sorry!

No, it's not an emergency. I just miss him and wanted to talk. You
say he's fine?

Well, thanks. I'll call back another time.

November 1995

The holidays are almost upon us; everyone is reminding me of how difficult it is going to be: our first Thanksgiving without you, first Christmas without you, etc. I can't imagine any one particular day being any harder than the other. Every day has been difficult in different ways. I can't imagine these being any different. We always had Thanksgiving at home, and anyone who was available was here. I have talked to the boys, and they would like to come to the house as usual. I look forward to having them and something to do that will keep me distracted. I enjoy working and being around my co-workers, but I particularly enjoy being at home. However, some days the aloneness is almost more than I can handle.

While talking at work about everyone's plans for Thanksgiving and where everyone was going, I was told that even though this would be a very difficult time for me and the family, we still had a lot to be thankful for. I replied, "I know what you are saying and yes, I do have a lot to be thankful for; however, this year I am not thankful and ask God for forgiveness!" I know He would understand.

Thanksgiving Day

Thanksgiving morning and I am busy in the kitchen. I have

made out the menu of things to prepare for dinner. It's funny. I have listed all the things that you liked so well and that I always fixed for you, and I have eliminated all the things I have always enjoyed. I guess they just don't seem important to me today.

I turned on the TV to catch a little of the football games; I know that is what you would be doing and at times I forget you are not here. Occasionally, I look towards your chair, expecting to find you sitting there; what are you doing, you are so quiet.

Everyone was here for dinner, and it went very well. We talked about how much we missed you and how you would have enjoyed the dinner. The evening was different in so many ways and was what we called "good different." Lying here tonight, remembering many other Thanksgiving nights, we would have talked about the evening, the dinner, the kids, and what foods were better than last year and those not up to standard. How I miss our late night chats.

"Thanksgiving" is written to commemorate our first without you; I daresay I cannot remember our first together, but I shall never forget our last together and the one tonight. I "am thankful" for the time we did have, if only brief.

Thanksgiving

Today we gather with our family and friends.

To sit around the dinner table and reminisce
of days gone by but not forgotten.

Thankful for the food we share,
prepared so lovingly.

Please pass the bread.

Thankful for the love of one another and for
one who exists in our hearts each day.

Thankful for our health and the gift
of life though ever so brief.

Please pass the potatoes.

Thankful for the sun that shines upon our faces
even at the bleakest hour.

Thankful for the rain that falls to cleanse
and purify our souls.

Please pass the cranberries.

Thankful for forgiveness and understanding
for one who lacks strength of heart
to give thanks today.

In a room full of emptiness, laughter echoing
from rooms long abandoned; I see your
smile, I feel your breath upon my face.

A single candle flickers in the night.
Casting an eerie shadow upon the wall.
A final reminder of desolation as it
slowly burns itself out.

Please pass the wisdom;
wisdom to find peace and understanding.

Please pass a candle; a candle to light
the way for we shall not walk in darkness.
Please pass. . . .

December 1995

    We made it through Thanksgiving and with the grace of God, we will make it through our first Christmas. I don't feel like decorating the house this year, but we did draw names and I will try to make Christmas bearable. I miss our shopping together; how much you hated to shop, but you always went with me if I asked and then you would get in the swing of things.

I will go to Mother's and Daddy's for Christmas Eve dinner, stay overnight, come home Christmas Day. Bobby and Marissa are going with me; Chris will spend Christmas Eve with your mother and cousins there. Mike and Martha will be with her parents. We will all have dinner together on Christmas Day.

I feel like I am in a daze most of the time; watching shoppers scurrying with last-minute buys. As you know, I generally finish my shopping early, but find I am also buying late this year. I can't stay focused and remember what I was going to purchase, so I have made more trips to the mall than normal.

The nights are the hardest; seeing the Christmas lights all around; parties, gaiety in the planning; excitement on the faces of the little ones. Everyone at work is so kind and thoughtful, without them I don't know how I would have survived these last few days. We had our office lunch and exchange of gifts, and I felt good until I came home to such bleakness. I think I will put some of my favorite ornaments out and just decorate with candles. I have been busy making Christmas ornaments for family, mostly to memorialize your passing. It will be doubly hard with Don also gone. I have made two ornaments to send to Mother for her tree—one with your name and one with Don's; we will have you there in spirit. I pray each day that I will survive your passing even though in my heart I want to be with you. I do know now that would be the last thing you would want. When my time comes, it will come; until then I must travel this road as best I can.

Christmas Day

It is almost midnight, another Christmas past. Everyone was here except Eli. He had the flu but asked that I send him a plate of food! How we missed you; I bought you another crystal fish for your collection. It will be the last one I will buy. I know you are laughing at me as well as being touched by my emotions; it is just too soon to let go and I feel better having a "wrapped" gift for you.

Lying here in bed, I am writing "Silent Night" to express how I envision your Christmas. How the heavens would have been decorated for all to see! I do wish you peace, and my gift to you is my love and my promise to make this transition. Your gift to me? Continue watching over me and the family, guiding and loving us as we struggle day-by-day.

Christmas is the celebration of the birth of Jesus. Somehow we seem to forget the real meaning as we exchange gifts and celebrate with one another. However, if only temporarily, I was able to find some peace and calmness within as I listened to various sermons on the radio reminding us of His birth and how much He loves and cares for us.

"Silent night, holy night, all is calm, all is bright . . . sleep in heavenly peace" shall be my comfort tonight.

Silent Night

Silent night, holy night,
A luminous sky ablaze with multitudes
of twinkling, shimmering stars
in flight.

How beautiful—your heavenly
Christmas tree.

Silent night, holy night.
A radiant sky holds fast; its silvery
moon gliding, swaying gracefully
till dawn's early light.

How beautiful—your heavenly
Christmas tree with its
glorious ornament atop.

Silent night, holy night.
Midnight descends as puffy clouds
hasten to unite; forming
circles, so pure, so white.

> How beautiful—your heavenly
> Christmas tree with its
> pearly wreaths all around.
>
> Silent night, holy night.
> Unwrapping your gift of love
> I now must hold within.
> Let peace be my blanket tonight.
>
> How beautiful—your heavenly
> Christmas tree adorned
> with such tender care.
>
> Silent night, holy night.
> All is calm, all is bright.
> Love in abundance was shared
> in our home tonight.
>
> May you now sleep, sleep
> in heavenly peace.

December 30, 1995

New Year's Eve is one day away, and I am becoming more and more anxious and agitated than over the holidays I have just experienced.

Although we spent many New Years with friends at the traditional New Year's Eve parties, the last few were spent quietly at home. We celebrated with a special dinner, a bottle of champagne, quiet music, and went early to bed, then up the next morning to watch all those football games.

I don't miss the festivities surrounding New Year's Eve, but rather look forward to a quiet night. I believe my anxiety stems from entering a new year not shared with you. Another stage/step of being forced to accept your death. Another reminder of time speeding past—images of "us" sometimes blurred. My fear is that they will escape me permanently and I will lose sight of you.

My New Year's Eve resolution is to do the best I can with what is left of my life, make some sense of it, and find out just where I fit into the scheme of things.

A resolution I made for you—don't forget where I am, remember to watch over me, and just "don't forget."

After listening on the radio to the New Year being rung in from different parts of the United States, I wrote "Auld Acquaintance."

Auld Acquaintance

"Should auld acquaintance be forgot?"
I ask as I sit here alone with the
new year fast approaching.

I shall quietly slip into this new year
as quietly as you slipped out.
Carrying with me much
apprehension and anticipation.

Apprehension of leaving a past
we shared, with only
memories my keepsake.

Anticipation of a life yet
to complete. To enfold a new
beginning until we are united.

As I listen quietly to the music
of the night—ringing in a new year,
I hear your voice of encouragement—
a melodious song within my heart.

I must go forward and decorate this
new year with heartfelt memories
and precious treasures so
carefully collected.

To go forward, following the light above.
Leading me to my journey's end
Leading me from darkness to
everlasting light.

I will go forward, for I have the
strength and love of one
who walks with me,
my trusted friend.

We must say good-bye to a year
filled with pain and sorrow,
to embrace happiness
and peace.

"Should auld acquaintance be forgot
and never bro't to mind?"

I think not.

January 1, 1996

I am excited and distressed but feel I am on the right track. I have decided to take our wedding bands to a jeweler and see if I can have them melted down. I will have my engagement ring resized for my right hand. Once I visualized what I could do, I immediately got in the car and drove to a jewelry store we had patronized and one I felt I could trust. As I hurried through the mall, almost in a full run before I could change my mind, I rounded the corner and as I entered the store I realized it was no longer a jewelry store! I backed out and looked around in a daze, wondering if I had driven to the wrong mall, so sure of myself. After standing outside and looking around for what seemed like eternity, I entered another store and asked what had happened to the jewelry store. I was told that the owner had died and the family sold the business; was this a sign that I was on the wrong track? Disappointed, I drove home. What to do?

I stewed over my dilemma for the rest of the day, so sure it was the right decision. I remembered the name of another family-owned jewelry store someone had mentioned; maybe I should go to them. The next day I made a phone call for directions and once again was on my way. When I arrived at the store, that old man "anxiety" followed me in and now my dilemma was "Can I do this, do I want to do this?"

A very nice young saleswoman assisted me and when I told her what I wanted to do, how I needed her to help me not only decide what I wanted but that it was the right thing to do, she immediately took charge. She showed so much excitement and enthusiasm that I was drawn in and forgot about my anxiety. We picked out a small puffed-heart design with a diamond in the middle. She told me it would be so beautiful and precious; I would have a keepsake to treasure and pass to family members. I left the store so elated I could hardly believe my good fortune. Where did this inspiration come from—relieving me of yet another burden? My therapist was right!

January 18, 1996

I have received a phone call that my hearts are ready for pick up and I am on my way! As the jeweler is approaching, I am holding my breath; I can't bear being disappointed. He has opened the first box. It is so small and shiny; the diamond twinkles as I peer into the box. My heart is pounding; they are beautiful.

Sometimes we struggle too hard to make sense out of what we want or need. We only have to be more confident in ourselves and stop expecting to be disappointed. I was so sure that having these hearts made was the right thing to do that I should never have put myself through so much agony and stress. I will try to trust myself in the future and follow my "heart."

Tomorrow night I will meet the kids after work and give Martha, Tara, and Marissa their hearts. They do not know what I have done, and I hope they will be pleased.

On January 18, my son Michael's birthday, I picked up four puffed hearts; one each for my daughter-in-law, my granddaughter, my future daughter-in-law, and my own. That night I wrote "Vows Unspoken." Now

I have something that will be as treasured as our wedding rings—the joining of our bands.

Vows Unspoken

He slipped a ring upon her finger.
To love and to cherish;
till death us do part.

She slipped a ring upon his finger.
In sickness and in health;
till death us do part.

Vows quietly spoken.
The joining of two hearts,
two souls.

A pledge of a lifetime together;
a pledge of undying love
never unbroken.

She slipped the ring from his finger.
I love you even more today.
Sleep now to awaken in peace.

She slipped the ring from her finger.
A lifetime of cherished dreams,
tears, and smiles.

So suddenly, calmly gone
but not to be forgotten.

She slipped the heart around her neck.

*How do I love thee . . .
I shall but love thee better after death.*
—*Elizabeth Barrett Browning*

February 10, 1996

I feel myself slipping back into a state of depression. Is this normal? How far forward must I go in order to return to the peace of mind I had worked so hard to obtain? As I sit here and compose this chapter, I have no idea where this will take me. This is yet another road untraveled. I had been told that as "time goes by," you get stronger and coping becomes easier. I believed that progress was indeed taking place, but today I am filled with dread. The crying is becoming intense again. Is the medication effective, is my tolerance fading, or could it be I am reliving the beginning of the end?

It's almost Valentine's Day; I can visualize our last Valentine's Day together as if it is playing on a screen before me.

February 14, 1995

Valentine's Day 1995 was a very special day for us. We went to dinner at one of our favorite restaurants (Thee Bungalow) to celebrate this special occasion; *we had a surgery date!* After all the waiting, testing, anxiety; surgery was in sight. You were so proud/excited; you couldn't wait to tell our waiter what we were celebrating.

It was also the beginning of a terrible nightmare. Before going in for dinner, you started having stomach pains. I asked if you wanted to go home and you said no, you would be all right. The pains subsided during dinner, and we thought they were gone. Unknown to us, it was the beginning of the breakdown of your immune system.

I was told that the first anniversary of your death would be difficult. However, I was also told that the holidays would be difficult. They were, but I survived. Why is this so different? Why do I feel like I am experiencing your death again but in a different role?

I cannot relive this nightmare. I must get some sleep. Just as my head hits the pillow and I settle in for the night, exhausted, emotionally drained, afraid, my eyes open and I feel I am in a trance. I know this feeling all too well; it will be another sleepless night such as I have experienced too many times before. I sit up in bed, pleading that this will go away. As tears stream down my face, I pound the bed with clenched fists and call out your name. I feel I have been here before; was it just yesterday or has it been longer? I cannot go back in time; I will not survive again.

As I reach out in the dark and turn my radio on, my voice in the night that I have become so dependent upon, I again find solace when desperately needed. The song they are playing is "Hushabye." I feel your nearness, and your message is loud and clear. It shakes me out of this trance, this state of nothingness. You have come to comfort me when I need you the most. In all our years together, you never let me down; I am not surprised tonight as I listen and hear a message I must follow.

I lie back down, calmly, serenely drifting off to another Valentine's Day we spent together.

February 12, 1965

You have proclaimed this day, as "Valentine's Day." You have just picked up the engagement ring that was ordered weeks before; and like a little boy, you can't wait to present it to me. You have made reservations at our favorite restaurant (The Derby). We have just been seated, and with a gleam in your eye, you slowly retrieve a small black box from your pocket. As a young, romantic girl, I had watched this scene in movies so many times before: soft lights, background music, champagne. It is all happening before me now and I am the movie star!

The ring you have chosen is so much like you—soft and delicate, yet shining like no other I have ever seen; unintimidating, yet majestic in its brilliance; unique, yet strangely familiar. A ring that I cherished the day you presented it to me and a ring that I will cherish until my days' end. Although I now wear it on my right hand, it is more of a loving reminder of something you picked out especially for me.

February 13, 1996

Today I am feeling stronger and have been able to sleep again.

In these last couple of days, you have given me the strength once again to accept your death and remember what we had together rather than what we do not have.

I borrowed lines from Elizabeth Barrett Browning to write "To My Valentine." I hoped to describe some of our daily/yearly rituals that may have annoyed each of us in small ways. You had a way of teasing me unmercifully rather than chastising.

To My Valentine

Roses are red, violets are blue
Each day of my life
Is filled with my love for you.

How did I love thee? Let me count the ways.
I loved thee to the depth, breadth, and height
Those dirty socks did reach, each
Time you tossed them across
The room, landing behind the hamper,
Waiting so lovingly for me to retrieve.

I loved thee to the level of every day's
Most quiet need, by sun and candlelight,
As we watched TV and you
Channel-hopped freely while striving
To avoid commercials, thus
Driving me to the brink of insanity.

I loved thee with the passion put to use
In my old griefs and with my childhood's faith.
When you told me the Easter bunny
Had died and I needn't color
Those damned eggs.

How did I love thee?
I still do.

Your little annoying habit of rolling up your dirty clothes in a ball and tossing them across the room, landing in the clothes hamper. On a good jump shot, you could land them in the hamper and close the lid in one swoop. More times than not, they landed (forgotten) behind the hamper where I retrieved them. And, you and those annoying remote controls! You couldn't stand to watch commercials and with a satellite, had many channels to hop to-and-fro. I remember trying to watch a football game, and when I looked away, I heard the referee announce a foul against a player. Just as I was asking when/why the rules had changed, I realized you had switched games; we were now watching basketball. Another evening we were watching a football game when a player was injured with a groin pull. Again, you switched channels to another football game and ten minutes later switched back just as the announcers were showing a repeat of the groin injury. I said, "Oh no, he injured his other groin!" I got this look and message, "Where have you been?" I quickly learned to go with the flow or better yet—keep up with the "remoting."

Every Easter I would color eggs for the boys, and this continued even after they had left home. One year I made Easter baskets for each of the boys and had them delivered at their work sites. You made fun of me and that was when you told me the Easter bunny had died and I need not continue with the egg business.

February 14, 1996

After completing "To My Valentine," I feel I have once again taken a step forward and must keep overcoming obstacles that get in the way. I know that is your message to me, and I will try with all my heart and soul to push forward in this healing process.

Valentine's Day is a special day for most people. It is now a day that I will remember as a time that was the beginning of our life together and a time that was the beginning of the end of our life together. We are about to complete the circle.

March 1, 1996

As I enter into March, I feel as if I am reliving your death. It is like watching a movie for the second time, one in which you don't like the outcome but have no way of changing it. I am living in a suspended state, walking in slow motion; you are alive and your impending death will be March 11, 1996. I know each day that you are going to die and there is nothing I can do; I feel like I am watching you die all over again; walking that long, lonely road while you lie helpless awaiting your journey. How am I to stand by and do nothing? Each new experience is more frightening than the one before.

The boys and I plan to meet after work on March 11, try to enjoy the evening and not dwell on the past. I know that is what you would encourage us to do. I pray each day that they are not experiencing this uncertainty, this unending agitation. With our love of one another, we will survive as we have so many times before since your death.

March 11, 1996

Well, today is here! I met family/friends after work. We shot some pool, had a beer, and shared memories of our life together, noting how you would laugh at our antics! It was a good evening.

It has been one year since you left me on my own. How many miles we have traveled in a year, yet gone nowhere. Your death is as vivid today as it was a year ago. This last month has been an extremely difficult one. I feel I have climbed the highest mountain, struggling to reach the top, knowing I must push on before I can reach that other side where the path is smoother, easier to walk alone.

One of our favorite songs was "Wind beneath My Wings." I so admired you and felt that you were the wind beneath my wings and that I did walk in your shadow. And now as I strive to walk in my own shadow, I will still have you beneath my wings, lifting me to heights I could never have reached had you not shown me the way.

I plan to end my therapy sessions—a year was my goal. I also plan to discontinue the medication at the end of this month. I pray that I will have the strength and courage needed to walk on, take what I have learned, and lean on my strengths to continue to my journey's end.

I have received several cards and letters from various friends and relatives to let me know they are thinking of me as we approach the ending of this first year. The other day I received a letter from Aunt EdnaLee with the following poem enclosed (author unknown):

Better to Have Loved

Do not let beloved ghosts return
To find that thoughts of them have
    Brought us to tears.
Let the dear memories glow and brightly burn.
Like friendly flames that banish from the years
    Our dark regrets.
Let each remembered one shape on our lips
    our fondest gallant smile.
To say, as they would wish, not,
    "You are gone."
But, "It was sweet to have you for this while."

I awakened very early this morning with "To My Beloved" forming in my head. I turned on the light, reached for my lap-top computer, and let it all spill out. Afterwards, I saw a message that I should live again and that you have not, will not, leave me; you are with me in so many ways. I need only stop and look, listen, and feel.

It is fitting to end this long year with "To My Beloved," a message from you to me as I have devoted this last year expressing my feelings to and for you.

To My Beloved

    Weep no more for me, my love,
For I have not left thee.

I am the rain that falls upon thy
garden walls. To cleanse and wash
away each yesterday.

I am the sun that shines upon thy face.
To embrace thee, to warm thee on a
golden summer's day.

I am the moon, the stars that shine so
bright. Leading thee, guiding thee
safely home each lonely night.

I am the wind blowing softly through the trees.
Listen ever so carefully and thou shalt
hear my voice.

I am the laughter within thy heart.
Open thyself once again to laugh, live
freely and joyously.

I am the loving within thy soul. Open thyself
once again to love, peace, and happiness
for all eternity.

I am the eagle that soars in the heavens above.
Open thine eyes and gaze upon me.
I shall lift thee up to soar once again.

Weep no more for me, my love,
For I have not left thee.

April 1996

Well, it has been two weeks since I discontinued my medication and once again I have hit rock bottom. I really thought I was ready, but I guess I was wrong; I am so disappointed. The doctor and I discussed my disappointment and he has reassured me that it is okay; I will try harder and set a new goal.

My last therapy session with Cyndee was today, April 30, 1996. I felt so many emotions during my session. When I walked into her office, I was sure it would be my last. In all of these sessions, I have fought with the devil, myself, and God; I have found myself again, and God has carried me all the way, leaving the devil far behind.

In summarizing my sessions: I reached my first goal—to end therapy after the first year; I had survived my ordeal, had hope for the future; I must continue one day at a time; and Cyndee was only a phone call away.

By ending my sessions, I have lost a friend but regained my freedom. I have felt like a prisoner in my own home, a stranger to myself, and a shell of a being. Unlike Humpty-Dumpty, we could put me back together again.

June 9, 1996

The day my husband died, I truly felt that I could not and would not go on with my life. I had no intention of ending it myself but felt it would automatically end on its own. How could life be so cruel and take something so precious from me, someone I was totally dependent upon and leave me behind to suffer for the rest of my life? How could a world exist without him? I would be called away as soon as I took care of things and his ashes were scattered. I had no doubt whatsoever that this was my destiny—to follow him wherever. I had often read that after the death of one spouse it is not uncommon for the other to succumb, and I honestly expected that to happen.

I have traveled a very long and lonely road to a destination that was often unknown and was unfamiliar from the start. I can truly say that I have now found peace within, I love Wally more deeply with each passing day, my faith has been restored and heightened, and my children remain by my side as steadfast as ever.

Today I travel in a new direction; less bumpy, fewer stops along the way, sunshine all around, and the tears in my eyes are for the joy I found in the love and friendship we shared for over thirty years. I am satisfied with the direction my life is taking me; albeit slowly, and actually look forward to many tomorrows. I am excited about starting over—creating the new me along with new and interesting hobbies, newfound friends and renewing old acquaintances; happiness is not far behind.

I will never forget Wally, nor am I expected to; and as I think of him every day, it is without pain but with joy and laughter. In my heart is where I will hold him now and hope he treasures our life together wherever his journey has taken him and that our brief life together had a purpose, which will be our legacy.

It has taken me a year to write this book and at times I wasn't sure I could finish it; I knew I would not be able to go on until I did. When I tried to sit down and come up with a befitting title, I was at a loss. While at work one day, the words "precious memories" suddenly flashed before me; I wasn't even thinking about the book. I turned to one of my co-workers and said, "I have just heard the title of my book." I frantically searched for pen and pad to write it down in case it disappeared as quickly. The title was so comforting and familiar, it just couldn't have been anything else.

After writing down my title, I remembered a hymn titled "Precious Memories," by J.B.F. Wright and Lonnie B. Combs. It was always one of my favorites growing up but long forgotten until this book. I believe it best sums up what I have tried to convey in my book.

This book has been rewarding and, at times, heartbreaking to write. We can find remembrance in every day without so much pain. We can take those memories and dwell on them until we suffer permanently or we can take those memories and hold them dear, share them, and relive them in a happy, positive way. "How beautiful, how precious is the peace that we can find in the legacy of memories our loved ones leave behind."

I hope you have enjoyed this book, found some peace, comfort, and even a little humor in my experience. Death, for those of us left behind, is often a terrible experience, one we will never completely get over, and oftentimes we'll feel so alone as we struggle through our grief. We are given the strength to find new life, new meaning, new purpose. We have only to ask, believe in ourselves, and love one another to rise above our misery, to embrace life once again.

If we listen, feel, and interact with our loved ones who desperately need us too, we will find that we are not alone. We are blessed with our loved ones around us here and now, and with those who have left us, they are never truly gone.

On this anniversary of the day we scattered my husband's ashes, I find it fitting to close this chapter of my life, our life. The circle is complete and will not be broken. And to my husband, "Forget Me Not."

Forget Me Not

As you pass so gently, quietly, to your journey's
   end.

Like a whisper in the night;
   a guiding light that shines so bright.

Like the fragrance of a rose;
   its breath flowing sweetly upon my nose.

Like the lightning in the sky;
   its thunder drowning out our final good-bye.

Like the silence in the room;
   to honor one who left too soon.

Like the battle so bravely fought;
   all I ask of you—*forget me not.*